111 Weird, Fun, and Random *Facts About the* UFC

*Inside the Octagon's Vault:
Unveiling 111 UFC Moments*

James Bren

Chapters

Chapter 1: The Birth of the UFC – 10

Chapter 2: The Mile-High Birthplace of the UFC – 14

Chapter 3: Royce Gracie's Triumph at UFC 1 – 17

Chapter 4: UFC 4 - The Introduction of Weight Classes – 20

Chapter 5: Chuck Norris, the Almost Referee – 23

Chapter 6: The Iconic UFC Octagon – 27

Chapter 7: The Compact Battlefield of the Octagon – 29

Chapter 8: Anderson Silva's Historic Middleweight Reign – 32

Chapter 9: The Historic Introduction of Women's Divisions in the UFC – 36

Chapter 10: Ronda Rousey: The First UFC Women's Bantamweight Champion and Liz Carmouche: The Pioneer of Female Fighters in the Octagon – 40

Chapter 11: Weight Classes in the UFC – 43

Chapter 12: The UFC's Global Reach – 47

Chapter 13: Georges St-Pierre - The UFC's Greatest – 51

Chapter 14: Jon Jones - The Reign of a Light Heavyweight Legend – 55

Chapter 15: The UFC Performance Institute - Where Fighters Evolve and Recover – 59

Chapter 16: Unified Rules of Mixed Martial Arts in the UFC – 63

Chapter 17: Fighter Weigh-Ins and Meeting Weight Classes – 67

Chapter 18: UFC Fight Outcomes – 71

Chapter 19: Recognizing Excellence - UFC Performance Bonuses – 74

Chapter 20: The Evolution of UFC Fighter Attire – 77

Chapter 21: Specialized UFC Gloves for MMA Competition – 80

Chapter 22: Notable UFC Referees - Herb Dean and Dan Miragliotta – 84

Chapter 23: The Iconic "Voice of the Octagon" - Bruce Buffer's Journey – 87

Chapter 24: The Crucial Role of Mouthguards in Fighter Safety – 90

Chapter 25: Honoring Legends - The UFC Hall of Fame – 93

Chapter 26: Hand Wrapping in the UFC – 96

Chapter 27: Scoring System in the UFC – 99

Chapter 28: The Sanitization Ritual of the Octagon – 102

Chapter 29: The Fighter's Crucible: Pre-Bout Medical Examinations – 105

Chapter 30: The Art and Peril of Weight Cutting in the UFC – 109

Chapter 31: Official UFC Fighter Rankings – 112

Chapter 32: PRIME Drinks and the UFC – 117

Chapter 33: Bruce Lee's Influence on the UFC – 119

Chapter 34: The UFC Video Game Series – 122

Chapter 35: The Power of Walkout Songs – 125

Chapter 36: "The Ultimate Fighter" - Forging Champions on Reality TV – 129

Chapter 37: Tito Ortiz vs. Ken Shamrock - A Fierce UFC Rivalry – 133

Chapter 38: UFC 40 - "Vendetta" - A Pivotal Moment in MMA History – 136

Chapter 39: The Octagon Mat - A Custom Canvas for Combat – 139

Chapter 40: Dana White - The Long Reign as UFC President – 142

Chapter 41: The UFC's Global Fan Base – 146

Chapter 42: The Art of Cross-Training in MMA – 150

Chapter 43: The Enigmatic Striking Style of Anderson Silva – 154

Chapter 44: The Diverse Spectrum of UFC Venue Sizes – 157

Chapter 45: The Grand Spectacle of UFC Opening Ceremonies – 160

Chapter 46: Conor McGregor - The Notorious One – 163

Chapter 47: The UFC's Worldwide Reach – 166

Chapter 48: The Art of Unique Fighting Styles – 170

Chapter 49: A Sport in the Crosshairs – 174

Chapter 50: The Rise of Interim Titles – 177

Chapter 51: Dominick Cruz - The Footwork Maestro – 180

Chapter 52: Diverse Origins, One Octagon – 183

Chapter 53: Unearthing "The Diamond" – 186

Chapter 54: UFC's High-Altitude Adventures – 189

Chapter 55: UFC 5 - The Superfight Showdown – 192

Chapter 56: UFC Fight Pass - A Gateway to MMA – 195

Chapter 57: From Octagon to Silver Screen - UFC Fighters Turned Actors – 198

Chapter 58: Inside the Octagon - Embedded Journalism in the UFC – 201

Chapter 59: The Art of Pre-Fight Trash Talk in the UFC – 204

Chapter 60: The UFC-WWE Crossover: Stars Who Shined in Both Worlds – 207

Chapter 61: Fighting Al Fresco: UFC's Outdoor Arena Extravaganzas – 210

Chapter 62: Decisions, Disagreements, and Controversies: Judging in the UFC – 213

Chapter 63: The Grand Stage: Fighter Entrances in the UFC – 216

Chapter 64: The Signature Walkout Attire of UFC Fighters – 219

Chapter 65: The Exemplary Sportsmanship of Georges St-Pierre – 222

Chapter 66: The UFC's Digital Realm - YouTube Channel and Beyond – 225

Chapter 67: Keeping the Octagon Clean - UFC's Partnership with USADA – 228

Chapter 68: Jon Jones - A Controversial Figure Beyond the Octagon – 232

Chapter 69: A Diverse Spectrum of Martial Arts in the UFC – 236

Chapter 70: Conor McGregor - A Meteoric Rise to UFC Stardom – 239

Chapter 71: UFC Across the United States - From Coast to Coast: The American Heartland of MMA – 243

Chapter 72: The Thrilling World of UFC Fight Night Events - Where Every Bout Matters – 246

Chapter 73: Unconventional Training Methods in the World of UFC – 249

Chapter 74: Fighter Safety and the Dedicated Medical Staff of the UFC – 252

Chapter 75: The Marquee Attractions - UFC Championship Bouts – 256

Chapter 76: Neil Magny's Remarkable Journey from the Military to the Octagon – 259

Chapter 77: The Power of Connection - Fighters and Their Social Media Presence – 262

Chapter 78: The UFC's Iconic Venue - Madison Square Garden – 266

Chapter 79: The UFC Hall of Fame Induction Ceremony – 269

Chapter 80: Fighters from Different Generations in the UFC - Early Days vs. Modern Era – 272

Chapter 81: Fighter Pre-Fight Rituals – 274

Chapter 82: UFC's Social Media Dominance – 277

Chapter 83: Fighters' Post-Fight Conduct – 280

Chapter 84: The Evolution of UFC Weight Classes – 283

Chapter 85: Unique Training Methods in the UFC – 286

Chapter 86: Fighter Safety and UFC's Dedicated Medical Staff – 290

Chapter 87: Championship Bouts as UFC Main Events – 294

Chapter 88: The UFC's Merchandise Line – 297

Chapter 89: Fighters Turned Coaches – 301

Chapter 90: Fighter Safety First - The UFC's Dedicated Medical Staff – 304

Chapter 91: Championship Bouts - The Epic Main Events of UFC Events – 308

Chapter 92: The Thriving World of UFC Merchandise – 312

Chapter 93: Celebrity Ownership in the UFC – 316

Chapter 94: UFC Fighter Safety and the Absence of Fatalities – 319

Chapter 95: Becoming a UFC Gym Owner – 321

Chapter 96: Record-Breaking Attendance at UFC 243 – 324

Chapter 97: Dana White's Continued Ownership of UFC Shares – 327

Chapter 98: UFC Fight Night 55 and UFC 224 - Record-Setting Finishes – 330

Chapter 99: UFC and the Unexplored Weight Classes – 333

Chapter 100: UFC's Strategic Investment in China – 336

Chapter 101: The UFC's Legal Battles – 339

Chapter 102: The Golden Legacy of UFC Belts – 342

Chapter 103: The Sound of UFC: "Face the Pain" by Stemm – 345

Chapter 104: Generational Clashes in the UFC – 348

Chapter 105: Joe Son - From Hollywood Villain to Real-Life Antagonist – 351

Chapter 106: Deciphering GSP's Chest Tattoo – 354

Chapter 107: Fighters Under Scrutiny - Post-Fight Conduct – 357

Chapter 108: Zuffa - More Than Just a Name – 360

Chapter 109: Tito Ortiz - Unveiling the Real Name – 363

Chapter 110: A Toothsome Proposition – 365

Chapter 111: Dana White Never Had a Pro Boxing Fight – 368

Closing Thoughts – 371

Other Books by James Bren – 375

Chapter 1: The Birth of the UFC

In the world of combat sports, few events have had as profound an impact as the creation of the Ultimate Fighting Championship (UFC). Established in 1993, this groundbreaking promotion was the brainchild of Art Davie, Rorion Gracie, and Bob Meyrowitz, each bringing their unique vision and expertise to the table. The UFC's inception was a pivotal moment that would forever change the landscape of martial arts and entertainment.

Art Davie: The Entrepreneurial Spirit

Art Davie, a martial arts aficionado and advertising executive, played a pivotal role in conceiving the UFC. His vision was to answer a simple question: "What would happen if you pitted martial artists from different disciplines against each other in a no-holds-barred contest?" This question would ultimately lead to the birth of the UFC.

Davie's entrepreneurial spirit was the driving force behind the UFC's creation. He believed that there was a market for a competition that would determine the most effective martial art. With a background in advertising, he possessed the skills necessary to promote and market this revolutionary concept to a broader audience.

Rorion Gracie: The Jiu-Jitsu Legacy

Rorion Gracie, a member of the legendary Gracie family, brought a wealth of martial arts expertise to the UFC. The Gracie family was renowned for their mastery of Brazilian Jiu-Jitsu (BJJ), a martial art that had proven highly effective in real-life combat situations. Rorion saw the UFC as an opportunity to showcase the effectiveness of BJJ against practitioners of other disciplines.

Rorion's involvement also brought credibility to the UFC. His family's reputation and success in the martial arts world lent an aura of authenticity to the competition. He saw the UFC as a platform to demonstrate the practicality of BJJ and to prove that technique could overcome size and strength.

Bob Meyrowitz: The Television Visionary

Bob Meyrowitz, a television producer and entrepreneur, was instrumental in bringing the UFC to a wider audience. His company, Semaphore Entertainment Group (SEG), provided the financial backing and logistical support needed to launch the first UFC event. Meyrowitz recognized the potential for the UFC to become a unique form of sports entertainment.

Under Meyrowitz's guidance, the UFC secured a pay-per-view deal with cable providers, ensuring that fans across the United States could watch the events from the comfort of their homes. This distribution model was groundbreaking and allowed the UFC to reach a broad audience.

The Birth of the UFC: UFC 1

With the combined efforts of Davie, Gracie, and Meyrowitz, the UFC held its inaugural event, UFC 1, on November 12, 1993, in Denver, Colorado. It was a single-elimination tournament that featured martial artists from various disciplines, including boxing, kickboxing, wrestling, and Brazilian Jiu-Jitsu. The rules were minimal, with very few restrictions, emphasizing the concept of "no-holds-barred."

The first event was a revelation in the world of combat sports. It showcased the stark contrasts between martial arts and provided thrilling, unpredictable matchups. Royce Gracie, representing Brazilian Jiu-Jitsu, emerged as the victor, demonstrating the effectiveness of ground-based submissions in this new form of combat.

The UFC's founders had succeeded in creating a spectacle that captured the imagination of fans and critics alike. Although met with controversy and challenges early on, the UFC's unique concept would prove to be the foundation for a global phenomenon that would revolutionize martial arts and combat sports.

As the UFC embarked on its journey, it would undergo significant transformations, adopting new rules, weight classes, and safety regulations. It would grow into a multi-billion-dollar industry, attracting the world's best fighters and captivating audiences worldwide. The creation of the UFC by Art Davie, Rorion Gracie, and

Bob Meyrowitz marked the beginning of a remarkable evolution that continues to shape the world of mixed martial arts today.

Chapter 2: The Mile-High Birthplace of the UFC

The Ultimate Fighting Championship (UFC), a global phenomenon in the world of mixed martial arts (MMA), had its humble beginnings in the Mile-High City of Denver, Colorado. The choice of Denver as the host city for the inaugural UFC event was no accident. It played a pivotal role in shaping the early history of the organization and setting the tone for what was to come.

Denver: The Unlikely Epicenter of MMA

In 1993, when the first UFC event was being planned, Denver was a somewhat unlikely choice for a groundbreaking combat sports spectacle. Known more for its beautiful Rocky Mountain scenery than for hosting cutting-edge sporting events, Denver was not on the radar of many fight fans. However, it had certain advantages that made it an ideal location for the UFC's debut.

No-Holds-Barred: The Early UFC Concept

The concept behind the first UFC event was simple yet revolutionary: to determine which martial art was the most effective in real-life combat situations. To do this, the UFC brought together practitioners of various fighting styles, including boxing, kickboxing, Brazilian Jiu-Jitsu, wrestling, and more. There were minimal rules, and combatants were allowed to use their full range of techniques. It was the ultimate test of martial arts supremacy, and it needed a venue that matched its boldness.

McNichols Sports Arena: The Birthplace of UFC 1

The McNichols Sports Arena, located in Denver, served as the venue for UFC 1, the first-ever UFC event. This unassuming sports arena, often used for hockey and basketball games, would become the stage for a revolutionary combat sports experiment.

On November 12, 1993, fight fans witnessed an unprecedented spectacle as martial artists from various disciplines squared off inside the Octagon. The circular cage, now synonymous with the UFC, made its debut in Denver. Inside this cage, competitors showcased their skills, and the audience was treated to an array of techniques rarely seen in a single event.

Royce Gracie's Triumph: A Brazilian Jiu-Jitsu Showcase

UFC 1 will forever be remembered as the night Royce Gracie, representing Brazilian Jiu-Jitsu (BJJ), emerged as the tournament's victor. Royce's success highlighted the effectiveness of ground-based submissions in this new combat format. His victories over larger opponents demonstrated that technique could overcome size and strength.

A Controversial Start: Challenges and Criticism

Despite the excitement generated by UFC 1, the event faced its fair share of controversy and challenges. Critics questioned the safety of the competitors, the lack of rules, and the potential for serious injury. This led to regulatory changes and additional safety measures in the subsequent events.

Denver's Legacy: The Birth of a Worldwide Phenomenon

Denver, with its hosting of UFC 1, holds a unique place in the history of the UFC. It was the city where the octagon-shaped cage was first introduced, where martial artists from diverse backgrounds clashed, and where Royce Gracie's BJJ skills shone brightly. This pioneering event set the stage for the UFC's incredible journey from a controversial start to a global sporting phenomenon.

In conclusion, the choice of Denver, Colorado, as the birthplace of the UFC was a pivotal moment in the history of combat sports. It was in this unassuming city that the UFC's founders introduced the world to a new form of entertainment that would go on to captivate audiences worldwide and change the face of martial arts forever.

Chapter 3: Royce Gracie's Triumph at UFC 1

When the Octagon was introduced to the world in Denver, Colorado, during UFC 1, it was designed to be a proving ground for martial artists of all disciplines. No one could have predicted that a slender Brazilian Jiu-Jitsu practitioner named Royce Gracie would emerge as the champion of this revolutionary tournament.

The Gracie Legacy

Royce Gracie hailed from the legendary Gracie family, known for pioneering Brazilian Jiu-Jitsu (BJJ). This martial art focused on ground fighting, submissions, and leveraging technique over brute force, making it a unique choice for an event where fighters with diverse backgrounds would compete.

The David vs. Goliath Scenario

In the inaugural UFC tournament, fighters came from various disciplines, including boxing, kickboxing, wrestling, and more. Royce Gracie, standing at just 6 feet tall and weighing around 178 pounds, appeared to be at a significant size disadvantage compared to some of his opponents, who were larger and more imposing.

The Tactical Advantage of Brazilian Jiu-Jitsu

Royce Gracie's approach to combat was fundamentally different from many of his adversaries. While other fighters relied on striking skills and brute strength, Gracie utilized the techniques of Brazilian Jiu-Jitsu to control and submit his opponents on the ground.

The Gracie Chokehold

One of the most iconic moments of UFC 1 came when Royce Gracie faced Ken Shamrock in the semifinals. The two fighters engaged in a grueling battle, with Shamrock attempting to use his wrestling skills to overpower Gracie. However, Royce executed a textbook rear-naked choke, forcing Shamrock to tap out and advancing to the finals.

The Finals: Royce Gracie vs. Gerard Gordeau

In the championship match, Royce Gracie faced Gerard Gordeau, a Dutch karate and savate expert. Despite a dramatic size difference, Gracie's strategy remained consistent—get the fight to the ground and submit his opponent. In a matter of minutes, Gracie secured a mount position and forced Gordeau to submit due to strikes, winning the tournament and establishing himself as the first UFC champion.

Royce's Submission Mastery

What made Royce Gracie's performance truly remarkable was his ability to submit opponents who outweighed him significantly. He showcased the effectiveness of Brazilian Jiu-Jitsu in real combat scenarios. His victories served as a testament to the importance of technique, leverage, and strategy in MMA.

The Impact of Royce Gracie's Victory

Royce Gracie's victory at UFC 1 not only solidified his place in MMA history but also helped popularize Brazilian Jiu-Jitsu and forever changed the landscape of mixed martial arts. His success demonstrated that size and strength could be overcome with skill and technique, a principle that still holds true in modern MMA.

Royce Gracie's triumph at UFC 1 was a watershed moment for the sport of mixed martial arts. His victories showcased the potency of Brazilian Jiu-Jitsu and set a standard for technique and strategy in a sport that was still finding its identity. Gracie's legacy continues to influence fighters and fans alike, reminding us that in the world of MMA, technique and heart can triumph over raw power.

Chapter 4: UFC 4 - The Introduction of Weight Classes

The early days of the Ultimate Fighting Championship (UFC) were marked by chaos and unpredictability. Fighters from various martial arts backgrounds stepped into the Octagon to prove their skills, but there was one glaring issue - the absence of weight classes. This lack of regulation often led to extreme mismatches and raised concerns about fighter safety. However, at UFC 4, a significant change was introduced that would forever alter the landscape of mixed martial arts (MMA) - the introduction of weight classes.

The Wild West of UFC

The first three UFC events were a spectacle to behold. With fighters of all sizes and disciplines participating, it was often a case of David vs. Goliath. The lack of weight classes meant that a smaller fighter could find themselves facing off against someone much larger and heavier. While this created a certain level of excitement and unpredictability, it also led to concerns about fighter safety.

Royce Gracie's Dominance

UFC 1 had been won by Royce Gracie, a Brazilian jiu-jitsu specialist. Gracie's submission skills and technique proved effective against larger, less skilled opponents. He further solidified his dominance by winning UFC 2 as well. However, the lack of weight classes meant that he didn't face opponents with similar size and skill sets.

The Need for Weight Classes

After UFC 3, which saw the emergence of another Gracie family member, Royce's brother, Rickson Gracie, there was a growing recognition that something needed to change. Fighters and fans alike saw the need for weight classes to create more balanced and competitive matchups.

UFC 4: The Turning Point

UFC 4, held in Tulsa, Oklahoma, on December 16, 1994, marked a turning point for the organization. It introduced the concept of weight classes, providing fighters with a fairer platform to showcase their skills. The event featured two weight classes: heavyweight (over 200 pounds) and lightweight (under 200 pounds).

The Impact of Weight Classes

The introduction of weight classes had an immediate impact on the quality of fights in the UFC. Fighters were now pitted against opponents of similar size and weight, leading to more competitive and evenly matched contests. This change not only made the sport safer but also increased its legitimacy as a true test of martial arts skills.

The Evolution Continues

UFC 4 was just the beginning of the UFC's evolution. Over the years, more weight classes were added to accommodate a wider range of fighters. Today, the UFC has multiple weight classes for both men and women, from strawweight to heavyweight.

UFC 4 was a pivotal moment in the history of mixed martial arts. The introduction of weight classes brought much-needed structure and fairness to the sport. It allowed fighters of all sizes to compete on a level playing field, paving the way for the growth and popularity of the UFC that we see today. This event marked a significant step in the ongoing evolution of MMA and its journey toward becoming a mainstream sport.

Chapter 5: Chuck Norris, the Almost Referee

In the early days of the UFC, the organization was a spectacle like no other. It was a wild mix of martial arts disciplines, no-holds-barred fighting, and a touch of the unknown. To maintain some semblance of order in the chaos of the Octagon, the UFC organizers needed referees who could handle the intensity of these fights. One name that surprisingly came up as a potential referee was none other than martial arts legend Chuck Norris.

Chuck Norris: A Martial Arts Icon

Before delving into the intriguing possibility of Chuck Norris as a UFC referee, it's essential to understand the man himself. Chuck Norris is a martial arts icon, known for his expertise in various disciplines, including Tang Soo Do, Taekwondo, and Brazilian Jiu-Jitsu. His impressive martial arts background and his role in countless action movies made him a larger-than-life figure in the martial arts community.

The Early Days of UFC: A Referee Dilemma

When the UFC was first established in 1993, the organizers, including Art Davie, Rorion Gracie, and Bob Meyrowitz, faced a significant challenge in determining how to officiate fights that featured competitors from diverse martial arts backgrounds. In the inaugural UFC events, referees with various martial arts experiences were used to officiate the fights.

The Chuck Norris Connection

During these formative years of the UFC, Chuck Norris's name was floated as a potential referee. Given his martial arts credentials and celebrity status, Norris seemed like a natural fit for a sport that was still finding its footing. Imagine the intrigue of having Chuck Norris in the Octagon, overseeing some of the most intense and unpredictable fights in the world.

Why Chuck Norris Didn't Become a UFC Referee

While the idea of Chuck Norris refereeing UFC fights is captivating, it ultimately didn't materialize. Several factors likely contributed to this missed opportunity.

Conflict of Interest: Chuck Norris was a well-known martial artist and a business owner in the martial arts world. Becoming a referee might have presented conflicts of interest or concerns about impartiality.

Logistical Challenges: Coordinating Norris's schedule with UFC events might have been challenging, given his film and television commitments.

Regulatory Considerations: In the early years of the UFC, there were limited regulations, and the roles of referees were somewhat fluid. It's possible that

Chuck Norris's involvement could have raised questions about the legitimacy of the sport.

Chuck Norris's Influence on MMA

While Chuck Norris never stepped into the Octagon as a referee, his influence on mixed martial arts (MMA) cannot be overlooked. He inspired countless martial artists and fighters, and his legacy in the martial arts community endures to this day. Many fighters have trained in martial arts disciplines, hoping to emulate the skills and presence of Chuck Norris.

Chuck Norris's potential involvement as a UFC referee remains a fascinating "what if" in the history of the sport. Although it never came to pass, the idea of the martial arts legend overseeing UFC bouts adds an extra layer of intrigue to the early days of the organization.

Chapter 6: The Iconic UFC Octagon

The Birth of the Octagon

The UFC Octagon, a symbol of mixed martial arts worldwide, had its origins in the minds of the UFC's founders. Art Davie, Rorion Gracie, and Bob Meyrowitz joined forces in 1993 to create a unique fighting spectacle that would set the UFC apart from traditional combat sports.

Art Davie's Vision

Art Davie, one of the co-founders, played a pivotal role in shaping the concept of the Octagon. His vision was clear: he wanted an arena that would not only provide a dynamic stage for fighters but also ensure their safety and fairness in every bout.

Collaborative Innovation

While Art Davie was instrumental in envisioning the Octagon, it's essential to recognize that the design and development of this iconic fighting space were a collaborative effort. Various individuals within the UFC organization contributed their ideas and expertise to refine the Octagon's design.

The Influence of John Milius

John Milius, renowned for his work in Hollywood, was associated with the early days of the UFC. While his exact role in the Octagon's creation remains a subject of discussion, it's clear that his involvement contributed to the Octagon's initial discussions.

The Octagon's Unique Design

The result of this collaborative effort was the UFC Octagon we know today. With its distinctive eight-sided shape, chain-link walls, and ample space for fighters to showcase their skills, it has become an iconic symbol of both the UFC and the sport of mixed martial arts.

A Symbol of Excellence

The Octagon is more than just a fighting arena; it symbolizes the UFC's commitment to innovation, safety, and providing fighters with a stage to prove their mettle. It's within this unique space that legends are born and where the pursuit of victory takes center stage.

As you watch UFC events, take a moment to appreciate the Octagon's rich history and its role in shaping the world of mixed martial arts. It stands as a testament to the collective vision and creativity that have forever transformed combat sports.

Chapter 7: The Compact Battlefield of the Octagon

Step into the world of the UFC, where combatants face off inside the enigmatic Octagon, a stage like no other in the world of sports. In this chapter, we'll delve into the origins, design, and significance of the Octagon, the hallowed ground where warriors test their mettle.

Origins of the Octagon

The Octagon, synonymous with the UFC, was born from the vision of the promotion's founders. It was conceptualized not only as a fighting arena but as a symbol of the fusion of martial arts disciplines. While its creation is often attributed to John Milius, celebrated filmmaker and martial arts enthusiast, it was the collaborative effort of various minds, including Art Davie and Rorion Gracie, that brought the Octagon to life.

The Unique Design

The Octagon's design is rooted in practicality. Its eight-sided shape ensures there are no sharp corners, providing fighters with a safe and level surface to showcase their skills. The canvas, emblazoned with the iconic UFC logo, bears witness to epic battles. Enclosed by a high chain-link fence, the Octagon offers both fighter safety and unobstructed views for spectators.

The Octagon Worldwide

While the Octagon was born in the United States, it has transcended borders. UFC events are held in arenas across the globe, each featuring the iconic Octagon as its centerpiece. From Las Vegas to Rio de Janeiro, and from London to Tokyo, the Octagon serves as a unifying symbol where fighters from diverse backgrounds converge.

The Octagon's Role in MMA Lore

Inside the Octagon, legends are made, rivalries are settled, and champions are crowned. It's a place where the unpredictable becomes reality and where the extraordinary unfolds. From thunderous knockouts to intricate submissions, the Octagon has borne witness to the full spectrum of human athleticism and fighting spirit.

The Unpredictable Arena

What sets the Octagon apart is its unpredictability. No two fights are the same, and the confined space encourages action. Fighters must adapt to the unique challenges it presents, making each bout an unforgettable experience for both the athletes and the fans.

In the Center of It All

The Octagon is more than a fighting arena; it's the crucible where fighters' dreams take shape. It symbolizes the essence of mixed martial arts, where diverse skills come together in a spectacle that captivates audiences worldwide. It's where heroes are born and where the indomitable spirit of MMA resides.

In the center of it all stands the Octagon, a symbol of the dedication, courage, and passion that drive fighters to step inside and compete at the highest level of combat sports.

Chapter 8: Anderson Silva's Historic Middleweight Reign

Anderson "The Spider" Silva is one of the most iconic fighters in UFC history, renowned for his incredible striking and unparalleled reign as the Middleweight Champion. For an astounding 2,457 days, Silva held this title, making it one of the longest championship reigns in UFC history.

The Birth of a Legend

Silva, born on April 14, 1975, in São Paolo, Brazil, started his martial arts journey at a young age. He began training in Brazilian Jiu-Jitsu and quickly excelled, earning his black belt. However, it was in the world of professional mixed martial arts that he would truly make his mark.

UFC Debut and Rapid Rise

Anderson Silva made his UFC debut on June 28, 2006, at UFC Fight Night 5. He faced off against Chris Leben and finished the fight in spectacular fashion, knocking Leben out in just 49 seconds. This emphatic victory signaled Silva's arrival as a force to be reckoned with in the UFC's middleweight division.

Championship Glory

Silva's rapid rise through the middleweight ranks led to a title shot against Rich Franklin at UFC 64 in October 2006. He made quick work of Franklin, winning via

TKO in the first round. This victory marked the beginning of Silva's historic championship reign.

Unparalleled Dominance

Over the next several years, Anderson Silva defended his Middleweight Championship against a who's who of the division. His unique blend of striking, precision, and charisma captivated fans worldwide. Silva's unparalleled dominance was characterized by his ability to finish fights with striking techniques that seemed almost otherworldly. His striking accuracy and defense made him a seemingly untouchable champion.

Classic Matches and Memorable Moments

During his reign, Silva participated in classic bouts against top contenders, including Dan Henderson, Chael Sonnen, and Vitor Belfort. These fights showcased his ability to adapt to different styles and opponents. Notably, his come-from-behind victory against Chael Sonnen at UFC 117, where he secured a triangle armbar submission in the final round, is still regarded as one of the greatest moments in MMA history.

Breaking Records

Silva's Middleweight Championship reign set numerous records. He holds the record for the most consecutive wins in UFC history, with 16 straight victories during his championship tenure. Additionally, his 10 consecutive title defenses are a record that still stands today.

The End of an Era

After more than seven years as the Middleweight Champion, Anderson Silva's reign came to an end at UFC 162 in July 2013. He faced Chris Weidman, who shocked the world by knocking out Silva in the second round, ending his historic championship run.

Legacy

Anderson Silva's legacy extends far beyond his reign as champion. He is often regarded as one of the greatest mixed martial artists of all time. His impact on the sport, both in terms of technique and entertainment value, is immeasurable. Silva's humility and sportsmanship outside the cage have further endeared him to fans and fellow fighters alike.

A Champion Remembered

Anderson Silva's reign as the UFC Middleweight Champion, lasting 2,457 days, remains one of the most enduring and celebrated chapters in UFC history. His remarkable journey from a young martial artist in Brazil to a global MMA superstar is a testament to his skill, determination, and charisma.

Anderson Silva's Historic Middleweight Reign commemorates the incredible accomplishments of a fighter who left an indelible mark on the sport of mixed martial arts and solidified his place among the all-time greats of the UFC.

Chapter 9: The Historic Introduction of Women's Divisions in the UFC

The world of mixed martial arts underwent a significant transformation in 2013 when the Ultimate Fighting Championship (UFC) took a groundbreaking step by introducing women's divisions. This pivotal decision marked a turning point in the sport's history, bringing a new level of excitement, talent, and diversity to the UFC.

A Milestone in MMA

Prior to the introduction of women's divisions, the UFC was exclusively composed of male fighters. While women had been competing in mixed martial arts for years in other organizations, the UFC's adoption of women's divisions was a watershed moment. It signaled a commitment to gender equality in a sport that had long been male-dominated.

The Rousey Era

The first women's division to be introduced was the bantamweight division (135 pounds), and it was headlined by none other than Ronda Rousey. Rousey, an Olympic judoka, had already established herself as a dominant force in women's MMA. Her fierce fighting style and charisma made her an instant star, and she quickly became the first-ever UFC Women's Bantamweight Champion.

A Champion's Dominance

Ronda Rousey's reign as champion was marked by her incredible dominance. She won her first six UFC fights via armbar submission, often in the first round. Her signature move became a symbol of her unstoppable force in the octagon. Rousey's ability to dispatch opponents with such consistency drew fans and media attention alike.

Expanding the Roster

The success of the women's bantamweight division opened the door for further expansion. The UFC introduced additional women's weight classes, including strawweight (115 pounds) and featherweight (145 pounds). This expansion allowed female fighters of varying sizes and styles to compete on the sport's biggest stage.

Iconic Fights and Legendary Fighters

The introduction of women's divisions led to some of the most memorable fights and fighters in UFC history. Rivalries like Rousey vs. Miesha Tate and Joanna Jedrzejczyk vs. Claudia Gadelha captivated fans worldwide. These matchups showcased the depth of talent and competitive spirit among female fighters.

Breaking Stereotypes

The inclusion of women's divisions shattered stereotypes and proved that female fighters were not only capable but also incredibly skilled and entertaining. The performances of fighters like Amanda Nunes, Valentina Shevchenko, and Zhang Weili further solidified the reputation of women's MMA.

Championship Pioneers

Throughout the years, the UFC's women's divisions have produced multiple champions, each with their unique stories and fighting styles. These fighters have become pioneers, inspiring the next generation of female athletes to pursue careers in mixed martial arts.

A Global Phenomenon

Women's MMA has grown into a global phenomenon, with fighters from all corners of the world competing in the UFC. It has given rise to international stars and showcased the diversity of talent in the sport.

Legacy and Inspiration

The introduction of women's divisions in the UFC not only transformed the sport but also inspired countless women and girls to pursue careers in mixed martial arts. Female fighters have proven time and again that they belong on the same stage as their male counterparts, and their performances continue to inspire fans worldwide.

The Historic Introduction of Women's Divisions in the UFC celebrates the pioneering spirit of the female fighters who have left an indelible mark on the sport. Their courage, skill, and determination have forever changed the landscape of mixed martial arts and continue to shape its future.

Chapter 10: Ronda Rousey: The First UFC Women's Bantamweight Champion and Liz Carmouche: The Pioneer of Female Fighters in the Octagon

The introduction of women's divisions in the UFC marked a historic moment in the world of mixed martial arts (MMA). It opened doors for female fighters to showcase their skills and compete on the biggest stage in the sport. Two names stand out prominently in this era: Ronda Rousey and Liz Carmouche.

Ronda Rousey: The Trailblazer

Ronda Rousey, often referred to as "Rowdy," is a name synonymous with women's MMA. She played a pivotal role in not only popularizing women's MMA but also becoming the first-ever UFC Women's Bantamweight Champion. Her journey to this historic achievement is a testament to her exceptional skills and determination.

Rousey's MMA career started long before her arrival in the UFC. She had already built a reputation as an armbar specialist in Strikeforce, where she held the Women's Bantamweight Championship. Her string of armbar victories was nothing short of remarkable, earning her a fan base and a reputation as one of the most dangerous fighters in the sport.

In 2012, the UFC president, Dana White, announced that the organization would be introducing a women's bantamweight division, and Ronda Rousey was destined to be a part of it. She made her UFC debut against Liz Carmouche at UFC 157 on February 23, 2013, in Anaheim, California. This fight, headlining the event, was historic for multiple reasons. It was not only the first women's fight in the UFC but also the main event, which was a monumental leap forward for gender equality in combat sports.

Rousey's fight against Carmouche didn't just live up to the hype; it exceeded it. Carmouche became the first female fighter to enter the Octagon, showcasing her tenacity and heart. Rousey, on the other hand, demonstrated her signature judo skills and determination. In the end, Rousey secured the victory via her patented armbar submission, retaining her title and solidifying her status as the inaugural UFC Women's Bantamweight Champion.

Liz Carmouche: The Pioneer

While Ronda Rousey made history as the first UFC Women's Bantamweight Champion, Liz Carmouche's role as the first female fighter to enter the Octagon cannot be overstated. She may not have left the cage with the championship belt that night, but she left an indelible mark on the sport.

Carmouche, known as "Girl-Rilla," brought with her a background in both MMA and the United States Marine Corps. Her relentless fighting style and resilience made her a fan favorite and the perfect opponent to face Rousey in the UFC's historic debut of women's MMA.

Her entrance into the Octagon that night signified a shift in the landscape of MMA. Female fighters were no longer relegated to competing in smaller organizations but were now given a platform to shine on the grandest stage. Carmouche's courage and determination played a significant role in making this historic moment a reality.

Ronda Rousey and Liz Carmouche played pivotal roles in the evolution of women's MMA within the UFC. Rousey's dominance as the first UFC Women's Bantamweight Champion and her signature armbar submissions made her a true pioneer for female fighters. Carmouche's fearlessness in becoming the first woman to step into the Octagon paved the way for countless others to follow.

Their contributions to the sport extended beyond their accomplishments inside the cage. They shattered barriers and inspired a new generation of female fighters, ensuring that women's MMA would continue to thrive in the UFC and around the world. The legacy of Ronda Rousey and Liz Carmouche is a testament to the enduring power of determination and the limitless potential of female athletes in the world of combat sports.

Chapter 11: Weight Classes in the UFC

In the ever-evolving world of mixed martial arts (MMA), the Ultimate Fighting Championship (UFC) has played a pivotal role in shaping the sport. One of the significant developments that has contributed to the UFC's success is the introduction of weight classes for both men and women.

Men's Weight Classes

When the UFC was founded in 1993, there were no weight classes. Fighters from various martial arts backgrounds, with significant differences in size and weight, would face off against each other in the Octagon. It led to intriguing matchups but sometimes resulted in vast disparities that raised concerns about fighters' safety.

To address these concerns and bring a sense of fairness to the competition, the UFC introduced weight classes for men. This move allowed fighters to compete against opponents with similar body sizes and weights, promoting a more level playing field. Over the years, the UFC has expanded its men's weight classes to accommodate a broader range of fighters. As of my knowledge cutoff in September 2021, these weight classes are:

Flyweight (125 pounds): The lightest weight class in the UFC, featuring fighters known for their speed and agility.

Bantamweight (135 pounds): Fighters in this division are known for their quick strikes and well-rounded skills.

Featherweight (145 pounds): This division includes some of the most exciting and dynamic fighters in the sport.

Lightweight (155 pounds): Known for its depth and talent, the lightweight division has produced some of the most iconic fighters in UFC history.

Welterweight (170 pounds): Often considered the most competitive division, welterweights are known for their blend of power and speed.

Middleweight (185 pounds): Fighters in this division are characterized by their strength and technical abilities.

Light Heavyweight (205 pounds): Featuring a mix of power and athleticism, this division has seen legendary fighters like Jon Jones and Chuck Liddell.

Heavyweight (Over 205 pounds): The heaviest division in the UFC, where fighters are known for their knockout power and size.

Women's Weight Classes

While the UFC initially focused on men's divisions, the demand for women's MMA was growing rapidly. In February 2013, the UFC made a historic announcement by introducing women's bantamweight as its first female weight class. The decision was heavily influenced by the rising star of women's MMA, Ronda Rousey.

The first-ever UFC Women's Bantamweight Champion, Ronda Rousey, was at the forefront of this historic change. Her incredible skill set and charisma helped propel women's MMA into the mainstream, and her rivalry with Miesha Tate and later Holly Holm became some of the most memorable moments in UFC history.

Over time, the UFC expanded its women's divisions to include:

Women's Strawweight (115 pounds): This division features fighters who are known for their technical prowess and relentless pace.

Women's Flyweight (125 pounds): Offering a more competitive space for fighters who fall between strawweight and bantamweight.

Women's Bantamweight (135 pounds): The division where Ronda Rousey made her historic mark, and it continues to showcase exceptional female talent.

Women's Featherweight (145 pounds): This division was introduced to accommodate fighters at a heavier weight class, and it has featured notable fighters like Cris Cyborg and Amanda Nunes.

These women's divisions have produced their share of iconic fighters, including Joanna Jędrzejczyk, Rose

Namajunas, and Amanda Nunes, who became a two-division champion by holding both the bantamweight and featherweight titles.

The introduction of weight classes for both men and women in the UFC has not only made the sport safer but has also allowed fighters to showcase their skills on a more even playing field. It has played a pivotal role in MMA's growth as a legitimate and widely recognized combat sport.

As the sport continues to evolve, there may be further changes and additions to the weight classes in the UFC, but one thing remains constant: the commitment to providing fans with thrilling and competitive matchups in various divisions.

Chapter 12: The UFC's Global Reach

The UFC, or Ultimate Fighting Championship, has undergone a remarkable transformation from its modest beginnings in the United States to becoming a global juggernaut in the world of mixed martial arts (MMA). This worldwide expansion is a testament to the organization's dedication to showcasing the sport of MMA on an international stage.

A Global Journey

Founded in 1993 in the United States, the UFC quickly recognized the potential for growth beyond American borders. The promotion's first international event took place in Yokohama, Japan, in 1997, signaling the beginning of its global journey.

Milestones in International Expansion

Throughout its history, the UFC has achieved numerous milestones in its international expansion efforts:

Canada: UFC 83 in Montreal (2008)

Canada played a pivotal role in the UFC's international expansion. UFC 83, held in Montreal, marked a historic moment as Georges St-Pierre, a Canadian fighter, won the UFC Welterweight Championship. This event solidified the UFC's presence in Canada, leading to a series of successful events in the country.

Brazil: UFC 134 in Rio de Janeiro (2011)

Returning to its roots, the UFC ventured to Brazil for UFC 134 in Rio de Janeiro. This event held particular significance as it marked the promotion's return to the birthplace of Brazilian jiu-jitsu and MMA. The event's success led to the establishment of a dedicated Brazilian headquarters for the UFC.

Europe: Nurturing European MMA Talent

The UFC's expansion into Europe played a pivotal role in the growth of MMA on the continent. Events in cities such as London, Dublin, and Stockholm introduced European fighters to the global stage and contributed to the surge of MMA's popularity in the region. Fighters like Conor McGregor and Michael Bisping emerged as stars, with McGregor becoming one of the UFC's biggest draws.

China: "The Ultimate Fighter China" (2014)

Recognizing China's immense potential as a major MMA market due to its vast population, the UFC launched "The Ultimate Fighter: China" in 2014. This reality TV series was designed to discover and promote Chinese MMA talent, representing a strategic move to tap into China's burgeoning MMA scene.

Australia and New Zealand: UFC Fight Night in Sydney (2014)

UFC Fight Night events in Australia and New Zealand have become fixtures on the UFC's calendar. These events have not only showcased the incredible talent from Down Under but have also seen fighters like Robert Whittaker and Israel Adesanya rise to prominence and eventually claim UFC championships.

Abu Dhabi: UFC Fight Island (2020)

The COVID-19 pandemic forced the UFC to adapt its approach to hosting events. This led to the creation of "Fight Island" in Abu Dhabi, a unique venue that allowed the UFC to continue hosting international events safely during the pandemic. This demonstrated the organization's adaptability and unwavering commitment to global expansion.

The Impact of International Expansion

The UFC's relentless international expansion has left an indelible mark on the sport of MMA. It has not only provided fighters from diverse backgrounds with opportunities to display their skills on a global stage but has also cultivated a diverse and passionate fan base. MMA has transcended cultural boundaries, uniting people worldwide through their shared passion for the sport.

The UFC's dedication to hosting events in various countries has not only expanded its reach but has also nurtured the global growth of MMA. It has given fighters the opportunity to chase their dreams and inspired countless individuals to take up the sport. As the UFC continues to broaden its horizons, one thing is evident: MMA's popularity knows no boundaries, and the UFC will remain a global powerhouse in combat sports for years to come.

Chapter 13: Georges St-Pierre - The UFC's Greatest

In the annals of mixed martial arts (MMA) history, certain names shine brighter than the rest. Georges St-Pierre, often referred to simply as GSP, stands as a beacon of excellence in the Ultimate Fighting Championship (UFC) and is widely considered one of the greatest fighters to ever step inside the Octagon.

The Early Years of GSP

Georges St-Pierre was born on May 19, 1981, in Saint-Isidore, Quebec, Canada. His journey to becoming an MMA legend began with a foundation in Kyokushin karate and Brazilian Jiu-Jitsu. As a young athlete, GSP's dedication to martial arts was apparent, and he soon began training in boxing, wrestling, and other disciplines.

UFC Debut and the Welterweight Division

Georges St-Pierre made his UFC debut at UFC 46 in 2004, competing in the welterweight division. He quickly showcased his potential by defeating his opponent, Karo Parisyan, and a star was born.

It was in the welterweight division where GSP truly cemented his legacy. His incredible work ethic, athleticism, and intelligence made him a dominant force. He went on a winning streak, defeating notable fighters such as Matt Hughes, Frank Trigg, and Sean

Sherk, earning himself a title shot against Hughes for the UFC Welterweight Championship.

First Title Reign: UFC Welterweight Champion

At UFC 65 in 2006, Georges St-Pierre faced Matt Hughes for the welterweight title. GSP's athleticism and skill proved too much for Hughes, and he secured a second-round TKO victory to claim the championship.

However, his first title reign was not without its challenges. At UFC 69, he faced a shocking upset defeat to Matt Serra. This loss served as a turning point in GSP's career, motivating him to become an even more complete and dominant fighter.

Redemption and a Legacy of Excellence

GSP's redemption arc is legendary. He reclaimed the welterweight title at UFC 83 in front of a hometown crowd in Montreal by defeating Matt Serra. This victory was a symbol of his resilience and determination.

Over the course of his career, Georges St-Pierre defended his welterweight title multiple times, consistently showcasing his unparalleled skill set. His fighting style was a testament to his well-roundedness, blending striking, wrestling, and Brazilian Jiu-Jitsu seamlessly.

Second Title Reign: UFC Welterweight Champion

GSP's second reign as UFC Welterweight Champion saw him defend the title against top contenders, solidifying his status as one of the greatest champions in UFC history. Notable victories included wins over Jon Fitch, Thiago Alves, and Josh Koscheck.

Despite his dominance in the welterweight division, GSP faced a question that lingers over many great fighters: "What's next?" In 2013, he decided to step away from the sport temporarily, vacating his title and citing personal reasons for his hiatus.

Return and Middleweight Pursuit

After a four-year hiatus, Georges St-Pierre returned to the Octagon in 2017. However, this time he had his sights set on a new challenge: the UFC Middleweight Championship. At UFC 217, he faced Michael Bisping and secured a victory via submission, becoming a two-division champion.

GSP's accomplishment was historic. He became only the fourth fighter in UFC history to win titles in two weight classes, joining the ranks of legends like Randy Couture, BJ Penn, and Conor McGregor.

Legacy and Retirement

In February 2019, Georges St-Pierre officially announced his retirement from MMA, leaving behind an unparalleled legacy. His record of 26 wins and 2 losses, along with his three UFC titles and numerous title defenses, solidified his status as one of the sport's all-time greats.

Beyond his accomplishments inside the Octagon, GSP's influence extended outside the cage. He was a consummate professional, a role model for young fighters, and an ambassador for the sport. His commitment to clean competition and sportsmanship set a standard for future generations.

The Georges St-Pierre Effect

Georges St-Pierre's impact on the UFC and MMA as a whole cannot be overstated. He showcased the importance of a well-rounded skill set, disciplined training, and mental toughness. His success inspired countless athletes to pursue careers in MMA and helped the sport gain mainstream recognition.

GSP's journey from a young martial artist in Canada to a global MMA icon is a testament to the power of dedication, hard work, and a commitment to excellence. His legacy will continue to shape the world of MMA for generations to come, reminding us all of what it means to be a true martial artist and champion.

Chapter 14: Jon Jones - The Reign of a Light Heavyweight Legend

In the world of mixed martial arts, certain fighters ascend to a level of greatness that defines an era. Jon "Bones" Jones, the enigmatic and dominant force in the UFC's light heavyweight division, is undoubtedly one of those legends. With a record-breaking number of title defenses and a unique fighting style, Jon Jones has left an indelible mark on the sport.

Emergence of a Phenom

Jon Jones was born on July 19, 1987, in Rochester, New York. His journey into the world of combat sports began with wrestling, and it was evident from an early age that he possessed the physical gifts and work ethic necessary to excel. He transitioned to MMA, making his professional debut in April 2008.

Jones' UFC debut came in August 2008 at UFC 87, where he faced Andre Gusmão. His unorthodox striking, combined with wrestling skills honed on the mats, immediately caught the attention of fans and fighters alike.

Light Heavyweight Ascension

Jones' rise through the ranks of the light heavyweight division was meteoric. His athleticism, creativity, and adaptability made him a unique and challenging opponent for anyone in the division. He quickly dispatched seasoned veterans and earned a reputation as a future champion.

At UFC 128 in March 2011, Jon Jones faced Maurício "Shogun" Rua for the UFC Light Heavyweight Championship. It was a historic moment, as Jones became the youngest UFC champion at the age of 23. This victory marked the beginning of his legendary reign.

A Reign of Dominance

What followed was a reign of dominance seldom seen in MMA. Jon Jones defended his light heavyweight title with remarkable consistency. His style was a fusion of striking, wrestling, and submissions, making him a formidable and unpredictable opponent.

Over the course of his career, Jones faced and defeated some of the division's best, including Rashad Evans, Quinton "Rampage" Jackson, Vitor Belfort, and Daniel Cormier. His unique skill set and adaptability allowed him to thwart various challenges and maintain his stranglehold on the division.

Breaking Records

In September 2011, at UFC 135, Jon Jones successfully defended his title against Quinton "Rampage" Jackson. This marked the beginning of a record-breaking journey. Jones would go on to defend his title 11 times, setting a new standard for title defenses in the light heavyweight division.

His remarkable run included wins over Alexander Gustafsson, Chael Sonnen, Glover Teixeira, and more. Each victory solidified his legacy as one of the sport's greatest champions.

Controversies and Comebacks

Jon Jones' career wasn't without its share of controversies. Outside the cage, he faced legal issues and suspension due to doping violations. These setbacks temporarily halted his fighting career and led to the stripping of his title.

However, Jones made a triumphant return in December 2018 at UFC 232, recapturing the light heavyweight championship. This comeback showcased his resilience and determination, proving that he could overcome adversity both inside and outside the Octagon.

A Legacy for the Ages

Jon Jones' legacy extends beyond his title defenses and remarkable fighting skills. He has inspired a generation of fighters with his work ethic and commitment to excellence. His analytical approach to the sport, combined with his physical gifts, has made him a true MMA innovator.

As of my last knowledge update in September 2021, Jon Jones had moved up to the UFC heavyweight division, setting the stage for a new chapter in his storied career. Regardless of where his career takes him, his impact on the sport of MMA is undeniable, and he will forever be remembered as a legendary figure in the history of the UFC's light heavyweight division.

Chapter 15: The UFC Performance Institute - Where Fighters Evolve and Recover

In the ever-evolving world of mixed martial arts (MMA), the physical and mental demands on fighters are continually increasing. To meet these challenges head-on, the UFC (Ultimate Fighting Championship) established the UFC Performance Institute, a state-of-the-art facility located in Las Vegas, Nevada. This institute represents a crucial resource for fighters, offering training, rehabilitation, and cutting-edge sports science services.

A Game-Changer for Fighters

The UFC Performance Institute, often simply referred to as "The PI," opened its doors in May 2017. From the moment it was unveiled, it became clear that this facility was going to be a game-changer for fighters across the globe. The brainchild of the UFC, it was designed to support fighters at every stage of their careers, from emerging talents to seasoned champions.

A World-Class Facility

The UFC PI is an expansive, world-class facility, spanning a massive 30,000 square feet. It houses a wide array of state-of-the-art equipment, sports science laboratories, medical facilities, and recovery areas. From strength and conditioning to nutrition, sports science, physical therapy, and more, the institute encompasses every aspect of fighter development and well-being.

Performance Optimization

One of the primary goals of the UFC PI is to optimize fighter performance. Fighters have access to a team of experts, including strength and conditioning coaches, nutritionists, and sports scientists, who tailor training and nutrition programs to individual needs. Cutting-edge sports science technologies are used to monitor performance metrics, ensuring fighters are continually progressing.

Nutrition and Weight Management

Weight management is a critical aspect of MMA, as fighters must meet strict weight requirements for their respective weight classes. The UFC PI offers nutrition counseling and support, helping fighters make the necessary dietary adjustments to compete at their optimal weight while maintaining their health.

Rehabilitation and Recovery

Fighters often face injuries and the wear and tear of rigorous training. The UFC PI provides world-class rehabilitation services to help fighters recover from injuries, surgeries, and the physical demands of the sport. Physical therapists and medical professionals work closely with fighters to ensure they return to training and competition in peak condition.

Research and Innovation

The UFC PI isn't just about providing services; it's also a hub for research and innovation in the world of combat sports. The institute conducts ongoing research projects aimed at improving athlete performance and safety. This commitment to advancing the sport benefits fighters and the MMA community as a whole.

Global Impact

While the UFC PI is located in Las Vegas, its impact is global. Fighters from around the world visit the facility for training camps, rehabilitation, and performance assessments. The knowledge and expertise gained at the institute are disseminated throughout the MMA world, benefitting fighters, coaches, and organizations worldwide.

A Resource for Fighters at All Levels

The UFC PI isn't exclusive to UFC athletes. It's open to fighters from various organizations and at different stages of their careers. Whether you're a young prospect looking to hone your skills or a seasoned veteran in need of rehabilitation, the institute welcomes fighters from all walks of MMA.

An Investment in the Future

The UFC's creation of the Performance Institute represents a significant investment in the future of the sport. It's a testament to the organization's commitment to fighter well-being, performance enhancement, and the continued growth and evolution of MMA.

The UFC Performance Institute in Las Vegas stands as a symbol of progress in the world of mixed martial arts. It's a place where fighters can evolve their skills, recover from injuries, and receive the support and expertise needed to excel in one of the most demanding sports on the planet. As MMA continues to evolve, the UFC PI remains at the forefront of innovation, supporting fighters in their quest for excellence.

Chapter 16: Unified Rules of Mixed Martial Arts in the UFC

The Unified Rules of Mixed Martial Arts (MMA) have played a crucial role in shaping the sport and ensuring fighter safety. These rules have been adopted by most MMA organizations, including the Ultimate Fighting Championship (UFC), and have helped bring legitimacy and uniformity to the sport. In this chapter, we'll explore the significance of these rules in the UFC and their impact on the sport of MMA.

The Need for Unified Rules

Before the establishment of the Unified Rules, MMA competitions often operated under a hodgepodge of regulations, varying from one promotion to another. This lack of consistency not only confused fans but also posed safety concerns for fighters. Fighters who competed in different promotions might have to adapt to different sets of rules, leading to potential misunderstandings and mismatches.

The Birth of the Unified Rules

The UFC and other major MMA organizations recognized the need for a standardized rule set. In 2000, New Jersey's State Athletic Control Board, under the leadership of Nick Lembo, took the initiative to create a unified rule system. These rules were aimed at maintaining the integrity of the sport while safeguarding fighters' well-being.

Key Components of the Unified Rules

The Unified Rules of MMA cover various aspects of the sport, including:

1. Weight Classes: The rules establish weight classes for fighters, ensuring that they compete against opponents of similar size.

2. Rounds: Fights are divided into rounds, usually lasting five minutes each, with breaks in between. Championship fights typically consist of five rounds, while non-title bouts have three.

3. Attire: Fighters are required to wear approved attire, including gloves, mouthguards, and groin protectors.

4. Fouls: The rules specify various fouls, such as eye gouging, biting, and groin strikes, which can result in point deductions or disqualifications.

5. Scoring: The 10-Point Must System is used to score rounds, with judges awarding the winner of each round 10 points and the loser 9 points or fewer.

6. Referee's Authority: Referees have the authority to stop fights if they believe a fighter can no longer intelligently defend themselves. This is crucial for fighter safety.

7. Weight Cutting and Hydration: The rules address weight-cutting issues and implement regulations to discourage extreme weight cutting and dehydration.

8. Octagon Rules: Specific rules apply to the Octagon itself, including its dimensions and requirements for the gate and padding.

9. Drug Testing: The UFC, in adherence to these rules, conducts strict drug testing to maintain a level playing field and ensure fighters' safety.

10. Judges' Criteria: The criteria for judging fights are outlined in the rules, emphasizing effective striking, grappling, aggression, and octagon control.

Impact on the UFC and MMA

The adoption of the Unified Rules had a profound impact on the UFC and MMA as a whole. It provided a structured framework for the sport to grow and develop while attracting a wider audience. With consistent rules in place, the UFC expanded into new territories and gained acceptance in jurisdictions where MMA was once banned.

The Unified Rules also made fighter safety a top priority. By clearly defining fouls and introducing weight-cutting regulations, the rules aimed to minimize the potential risks associated with the sport. This helped in improving the overall image of MMA and attracting high-level athletes to the UFC.

Moreover, the rules brought an element of fairness to the judging process. The 10-Point Must System, along with defined judging criteria, reduced the subjectivity of scoring and enhanced the transparency of fight outcomes.

The Unified Rules of Mixed Martial Arts have been instrumental in shaping the UFC and the sport of MMA. They have contributed to the growth, acceptance, and safety of the sport while ensuring fair competition among fighters. As the UFC continues to evolve, these rules remain a cornerstone of the organization's commitment to excellence and integrity in mixed martial arts.

Chapter 17: Fighter Weigh-Ins and Meeting Weight Classes

In the world of professional mixed martial arts, success often comes down to more than just skill and technique; it's a matter of precision, discipline, and strategy. One of the most crucial aspects of a fighter's preparation is making weight for their designated weight class. The weigh-in process is a highly anticipated and sometimes dramatic event leading up to a UFC fight, as fighters aim to tip the scales at their prescribed weight while maintaining peak physical condition. This chapter delves into the intricacies of fighter weigh-ins and how they contribute to the UFC's competitive landscape.

The Weight Class System

The concept of weight classes in combat sports has a long history, dating back to ancient Olympic games and the gladiatorial contests of Rome. However, it was not until the advent of modern mixed martial arts and the UFC that weight classes became formalized and consistent across promotions. Weight classes serve several essential purposes in the sport:

Fair Competition: Weight classes ensure fighters are relatively evenly matched in terms of size and strength. This promotes competitive fairness and reduces the risk of severe weight disparities leading to injuries.

Strategic Advantage: Fighters can optimize their training, nutrition, and conditioning for their specific weight class, enhancing their chances of victory.

Championship Opportunities: Each weight class has its own title, which fighters can vie for. Winning a title is often considered the pinnacle of a fighter's career.

The Drama of Weigh-Ins

Weigh-ins are a prominent part of the UFC event buildup and typically occur on the day before the actual fight. These events are open to the public and often take place in a large arena or a convention center, providing fans with a unique opportunity to see their favorite fighters up close and personal.

One of the most exciting aspects of weigh-ins is the face-off between the fighters. After successfully making weight, fighters step onto the scale, where their weight is announced. They then face off with their opponent for intense photo opportunities. These face-offs can become quite heated, serving as a preview of the intensity to come in the Octagon. Fighters use this moment to assert their dominance and engage in psychological warfare, attempting to gain any psychological edge over their opponent.

Making Weight

Making weight is a complex process that begins long before the actual weigh-in day. Fighters often work with nutritionists and dieticians to ensure they are gradually losing weight in a healthy and sustainable manner. Extreme methods, such as dehydration, saunas, and sweat suits, are discouraged as they can lead to severe health issues.

The fighter's official weight is determined by a certified scale, and they must meet or come under the designated weight for their division. If a fighter fails to make weight, they may be subject to fines and other penalties, depending on the circumstances and the athletic commission overseeing the event. Additionally, the fight itself could be in jeopardy if the weight discrepancy is too significant.

Rehydration and Recovery

After successfully making weight, fighters immediately begin the process of rehydration and recovery. Depriving the body of fluids and nutrients during the weight-cutting process can leave fighters feeling weak and drained. To regain their strength, they rehydrate with carefully balanced electrolyte solutions and consume a carefully planned post-weigh-in meal.

This process is crucial for fighters to enter the Octagon in peak physical condition. Rapid rehydration and recovery can be a decisive factor in a fighter's performance and overall well-being during the fight.

Weigh-In Spectacles

Over the years, weigh-ins have become elaborate spectacles, often featuring live music, pyrotechnics, and elaborate stage setups. The goal is to engage fans, build excitement, and generate interest in the upcoming event. The UFC understands that weigh-ins serve as a critical promotional tool and a way to connect with fans on a personal level.

Fighter weigh-ins are not just a formality but a fundamental part of the UFC's competitive structure. They ensure that fighters are appropriately matched, promote fair competition, and add an element of drama and anticipation to the lead-up of each event. The process of making weight and the subsequent rehydration are critical aspects of a fighter's preparation, significantly impacting their performance inside the Octagon.

Chapter 18: UFC Fight Outcomes

In the electrifying world of the Ultimate Fighting Championship (UFC), battles can reach their conclusion through a myriad of ways. Unlike many other combat sports, the UFC offers a wide array of potential outcomes, each adding its unique flavor to the fight game's drama. Let's delve into the various ways a UFC fight can reach its decisive end.

Knockout (KO): Among the most exhilarating conclusions to a UFC bout is the knockout. This spectacle unfolds when a fighter delivers a powerful strike that incapacitates their opponent, rendering them unconscious and unable to continue the battle. Knockouts can result from punches, kicks, elbows, or even knees, offering fans breathtaking moments and unforgettable highlights.

Submission (Sub): Submissions are a testament to a fighter's grappling prowess. A fighter secures victory by submission when they skillfully apply a joint lock or a chokehold that compels their adversary to concede defeat. These intricate maneuvers showcase the technical aspect of the sport, offering a contrast to the striking exchanges that often dominate the spotlight.

Decision (Dec): When the final horn sounds, and neither fighter has been knocked out or submitted, the bout goes to the judges' scorecards. This marks the emergence of a decision victory, where the three cage-side judges evaluate the entire contest's performance.

Fighters accumulate points through effective striking, grappling, and octagon control. The outcome is determined by unanimous decision, split decision, or majority decision.

Technical Knockout (TKO): A technical knockout represents an outcome where a fighter is deemed unable to continue the contest due to an accumulation of damage or an injury. The referee plays a pivotal role in a TKO finish, ensuring the fighter's safety by stepping in when necessary. This can happen when a fighter is no longer intelligently defending themselves or is suffering from severe damage.

Doctor's Stoppage (Doc Stop): Sometimes, the octagon physician becomes an instrumental figure in a UFC fight's conclusion. If a fighter sustains an injury or shows signs of physical distress, the ringside doctor may intervene, advising the referee to stop the bout to protect the fighter's well-being.

Disqualification (DQ): In the rare instance of a flagrant violation of the rules, a fighter may be disqualified. This means their opponent is declared the victor due to the egregious breach of regulations, often resulting from illegal strikes or actions.

No Contest (NC): Occasionally, unforeseen circumstances can lead to a fight being declared a no contest. This could result from accidental eye pokes, groin strikes, or other occurrences that prevent a fair and conclusive outcome.

Submission to Strikes (STS): A fighter might concede defeat by verbally tapping or signaling to the referee when they are overwhelmed by their opponent's strikes. This happens when a fighter has taken substantial damage and acknowledges their inability to continue.

In the dynamic world of the UFC, these various outcomes keep fans on the edge of their seats, showcasing the diversity of skills and strategies employed by fighters as they aim to secure victory. Each fight is a unique journey, offering its narrative and culminating in one of these exciting outcomes, making every bout an unforgettable spectacle for fans worldwide.

Chapter 19: Recognizing Excellence - UFC Performance Bonuses

In the high-stakes world of mixed martial arts, the UFC has found a unique way to reward fighters for their exceptional performances and memorable moments inside the octagon. The introduction of performance bonuses has not only incentivized fighters to give their all but has also added an extra layer of excitement for fans. Two of the most coveted awards in the UFC are the "Fight of the Night" and "Performance of the Night" bonuses.

Fight of the Night: Celebrating Battles of Grit and Determination

"Fight of the Night" bonuses are awarded to the fighters who put on the most captivating and entertaining bout of the evening. These awards recognize the heart, determination, and sportsmanship displayed by the fighters as they engage in fierce combat. "Fight of the Night" bonuses often go to matchups that go the distance, showcasing incredible striking exchanges, grappling wars, and moments of sheer resilience.

These bonuses serve as a nod to the fighters who not only win their battles but do so in a manner that captivates the audience. Fans remember these fights for years to come, and fighters often consider earning a "Fight of the Night" bonus as a badge of honor. It's not just about victory; it's about pushing one's limits and creating moments that MMA enthusiasts will never forget.

Performance of the Night: Highlighting Exceptional Individual Showings

In addition to celebrating the back-and-forth wars that captivate audiences, the UFC also recognizes individual excellence with "Performance of the Night" bonuses. These awards are presented to fighters who deliver outstanding, jaw-dropping displays of skill, technique, and dominance during their bouts.

A "Performance of the Night" bonus can be earned by a fighter who achieves a remarkable knockout, secures a lightning-fast submission, or dominates their opponent in a manner that leaves no doubt about their superiority. These bonuses reflect not only a fighter's victory but their ability to shine brighter than all others on that particular fight night.

Impact on Fighters and the Sport

The introduction of performance bonuses has had a profound impact on the UFC and the sport of mixed martial arts as a whole. It motivates fighters to aim for more than just a win; they strive for excellence in every aspect of their performance. The pursuit of these bonuses often leads to more exciting, technically impressive, and memorable fights.

Fighters understand that a "Fight of the Night" or "Performance of the Night" bonus not only brings financial rewards but also elevates their status in the sport. It can lead to increased popularity, more significant opportunities, and a place in the hearts of fans worldwide.

These bonuses have become an integral part of the UFC's identity, generating buzz before and after events as fans speculate on which fighters will be recognized for their remarkable performances. It's not uncommon for fighters to push their limits and take risks in pursuit of these coveted awards, and this drive for excellence benefits the sport as a whole.

The UFC's introduction of performance bonuses like "Fight of the Night" and "Performance of the Night" has added an extra layer of excitement and motivation to the world of mixed martial arts. These bonuses celebrate the heart, skill, and determination of fighters while elevating the overall quality of the sport, ensuring that fans are treated to unforgettable moments inside the octagon.

Chapter 20: The Evolution of UFC Fighter Attire

The world of mixed martial arts has witnessed significant changes in fighter attire over the years. Fighters' clothing, once adorned with various sponsors' logos, underwent a transformation with the introduction of exclusive apparel partnerships. This chapter explores the evolution of UFC fighter attire, from the era of individual sponsorships to the Reebok deal and the subsequent transition to Venum.

The Sponsorship Era: Fighters as Human Billboards

In the early days of the UFC, fighters' attire was like a canvas for sponsors. Fighters would walk into the octagon wearing shorts, walkout shirts, and even hats plastered with logos and brand names. This was a symbiotic relationship, with fighters earning income from sponsorships while brands gained exposure to a global audience.

These sponsorships often showcased fighters' individuality and unique affiliations. It was not uncommon to see fighters from diverse backgrounds with sponsors ranging from local businesses to major international brands. The colorful and diverse array of sponsor logos on fighters' attire became part of the visual tapestry of the sport.

The Reebok Era: Standardization and the UFC Uniform

In 2015, the UFC announced a groundbreaking partnership with Reebok, marking a significant shift in fighter attire. The deal aimed to standardize fighter uniforms, creating a more professional and consistent look for the organization. Under the Reebok era, fighters received a predetermined payout based on their experience level and number of UFC fights. This arrangement aimed to provide financial security but also faced criticism for limiting fighters' earning potential compared to individual sponsorships.

The introduction of the Reebok uniform brought about a more corporate and standardized appearance. Fighters wore Reebok-branded shorts and shirts featuring the UFC logo. While it eliminated the visual clutter of numerous sponsor logos, it also took away the unique, personalized touch of fighter attire. Fighters' identities were no longer expressed through their clothing choices.

The Venum Era: A New Era of Fighter Attire

In 2021, the UFC transitioned from its partnership with Reebok to a new deal with Venum. This marked a shift towards more fighter-centric attire. Venum introduced a line of fight kits that retained the professional look while allowing for personalization. Fighters could choose their walkout music, and their fight kits featured their names and country flags, providing a more individualized touch compared to the Reebok era.

The Venum era offers fighters a chance to regain some of their individuality and brand themselves in unique ways. While the UFC maintains its corporate partnership with Venum, fighters now have more control over their appearance, allowing them to connect with fans on a personal level.

The Impact on Fighters and the UFC

The evolution of fighter attire reflects the UFC's journey from a niche sport to a global phenomenon. The transition from sponsor-heavy attire to standardized uniforms and, eventually, to personalized fight kits represents the UFC's commitment to professionalism and athlete branding.

Each era had its advantages and drawbacks. While sponsorships allowed fighters to earn more income, standardized uniforms brought a more corporate and professional image to the sport. The Venum era seeks to strike a balance by offering fighters some personalization within the framework of a corporate partnership.

The evolution of UFC fighter attire mirrors the sport's growth and transformation over the years, reflecting the UFC's commitment to providing fighters with opportunities for financial security and personal branding while maintaining a professional and consistent image.

Chapter 21: Specialized UFC Gloves for MMA Competition

When it comes to mixed martial arts (MMA), every detail counts, and one of the most crucial aspects of fighter gear is the gloves. In the UFC, gloves are not just ordinary hand coverings; they are highly specialized tools designed to maximize both fighter safety and performance.

The Early Days of UFC Gloves

In the early days of the UFC, fighters didn't have the benefit of the advanced gloves seen in today's Octagon. In fact, there were minimal regulations regarding the gloves worn by competitors. Fighters often used open-fingered gloves or even opted for the thin, fingerless gloves typically used in traditional martial arts. These early gloves offered limited protection, and fighters had to be cautious to avoid injuring their own hands while delivering powerful strikes.

The Evolution of UFC Gloves

As the sport of MMA grew in popularity and legitimacy, the need for improved safety measures became evident. The UFC, along with other MMA organizations, recognized that better gloves were a necessity. This led to the development of specialized MMA gloves, designed to address several critical aspects:

1. Hand Protection: UFC gloves are padded to protect the fighter's hands. The padding is strategically placed over the knuckles and fingers to minimize the risk of fractures or injuries during strikes.

2. Wrist Support: MMA gloves provide essential wrist support. The wrist area is reinforced and often includes an adjustable strap to secure the glove firmly in place. This support helps stabilize the wrist joint during grappling and striking.

3. Finger Mobility: Unlike traditional boxing gloves, which keep the fingers enclosed in a fist-like position, MMA gloves allow for more finger mobility. This design is essential for grappling, as fighters need to grip, control, and submit their opponents.

4. Lightweight Design: UFC gloves are intentionally lightweight to allow fighters to move their hands and arms freely. This design is crucial for quick strikes, counters, and grappling maneuvers.

5. Padding Density: The padding inside UFC gloves is carefully chosen for its density. It provides protection without compromising the fighter's ability to feel and control their strikes.

6. Thumb Positioning: A key feature of MMA gloves is the positioning of the thumb. Unlike boxing gloves, where the thumb is often tucked in, MMA gloves have the thumb in a more extended position. This allows for a better grip and enhances the fighter's ability to secure submissions.

7. Durable Materials: UFC gloves are constructed from durable materials to withstand the rigors of training and competition. They are designed to last through intense workouts and multiple fights.

8. Branding and Sponsorship: Over the years, the appearance of UFC gloves has evolved to incorporate branding and sponsorship logos. This has become an essential part of a fighter's gear, as it allows them to showcase their sponsors.

Regulations and Standardization

The UFC has stringent regulations in place to ensure that all fighters wear approved gloves during their bouts. This standardization is critical for fighter safety and maintaining a level playing field. The gloves used in UFC events are typically produced by reputable manufacturers and are thoroughly inspected before each fight.

Fighter Preferences

While UFC gloves have a standardized design, some fighters may have slight preferences for the fit or feel of their gloves. UFC provides options for fighters to choose gloves that best suit their preferences, as long as they meet the organization's safety standards.

UFC gloves have come a long way from the early days of the sport. They are now highly specialized, designed to provide the necessary protection for fighters while allowing them the flexibility and mobility required to compete at the highest level of mixed martial arts. These gloves are a symbol of the evolution and ongoing commitment to safety and performance in the UFC.

Chapter 22: Notable UFC Referees - Herb Dean and Dan Miragliotta

In the world of mixed MMA, referees play a crucial role in ensuring the safety and fairness of the fights. Among the notable figures in the Ultimate Fighting Championship (UFC) as referees are Herb Dean and Dan Miragliotta. These two officials have become synonymous with the UFC, gaining recognition for their exceptional work inside the Octagon.

Herb Dean: "Big" John's Successor

Herb Dean, often referred to as the "Big" John McCarthy of his generation, is one of the most respected referees in the UFC. Born on September 30, 1970, in Pasadena, California, Dean initially pursued a career in law enforcement before transitioning into the world of MMA refereeing.

Dean's journey to becoming a prominent UFC referee began when he trained in Brazilian Jiu-Jitsu (BJJ). His martial arts background, combined with his experience as a fighter and law enforcement officer, provided him with a unique perspective on officiating fights.

He gained recognition for his calm and composed demeanor inside the Octagon, always prioritizing the safety of the fighters. Dean is known for giving fighters a fair chance to recover from difficult situations and for his precise decision-making during fights.

One of the most iconic moments in Herb Dean's career came during UFC 48 in 2004 when he officiated the fight between Frank Mir and Tim Sylvia for the UFC Heavyweight Championship. Mir secured an armbar on Sylvia, resulting in a gruesome arm break. Dean's quick intervention to stop the fight and protect Sylvia from further injury remains a testament to his dedication to fighter safety.

Over the years, Herb Dean has officiated countless UFC bouts, including high-profile championship fights and legendary matchups. His expertise, coupled with his level-headed approach to refereeing, has earned him the admiration of fighters, fans, and fellow officials alike.

Dan Miragliotta: The Giant of Officiating

Dan Miragliotta, known for his imposing size and deep voice, is another prominent figure in the world of UFC refereeing. Born on July 11, 1962, in New Jersey, Miragliotta brings a unique presence to the Octagon.

Before his career as a referee, Miragliotta was involved in martial arts as a student and eventually as an instructor. This experience laid the foundation for his transition into officiating MMA fights. His robust physique and commanding presence make him easily recognizable to UFC fans worldwide.

One of Miragliotta's standout qualities as a referee is his ability to maintain control during intense moments in a fight. His commanding voice and assertive gestures help him manage fighters and ensure that the rules are followed. This presence can be particularly important in the UFC, where emotions often run high.

Miragliotta has refereed a wide range of fights, from undercard bouts to championship clashes. His consistency and commitment to upholding the rules have made him a trusted figure in the sport. Fighters appreciate his fair approach and dedication to ensuring their safety.

The Evolution of UFC Refereeing

The role of referees in the UFC has evolved significantly since the early days of the sport. Herb Dean and Dan Miragliotta, among others, have played a crucial part in shaping this evolution. Their dedication to fighter safety and their ability to make split-second decisions in high-pressure situations have made them invaluable assets to the UFC.

As the sport continues to grow and evolve, referees like Herb Dean and Dan Miragliotta remain instrumental in maintaining the integrity of the UFC. Their presence inside the Octagon assures fighters and fans alike that the fights will be officiated with fairness, expertise, and a commitment to safety.

The legacy of these two remarkable referees will undoubtedly endure in the annals of MMA history, as they continue to contribute to the success and safety of the UFC and the sport as a whole.

Chapter 23: The Iconic "Voice of the Octagon" - Bruce Buffer's Journey

In the world of mixed martial arts, there are few voices as recognizable and iconic as that of Bruce Buffer. He is often referred to as the "Voice of the Octagon," and his passionate, energetic, and electrifying introductions have become an integral part of the UFC experience. But how did Bruce Buffer land the coveted job of being the UFC's official ring announcer? His journey to this role is a fascinating tale of passion, determination, and a little bit of family connection.

Early Life and Introduction to Announcing

Bruce Buffer was born on May 21, 1957, in Tulsa, Oklahoma. From a young age, he was drawn to the world of announcing and entertainment. His half-brother, Michael Buffer, had already made a name for himself as a renowned boxing and wrestling announcer. Michael's famous catchphrase, "Let's get ready to rumble!" had become a pop culture sensation.

Growing up, Bruce Buffer admired his half-brother's success and developed a passion for announcing. He initially ventured into various fields, including acting, modeling, and even as a professional kickboxer. However, his true calling remained in the world of announcing, and he was determined to make his mark.

The Meeting That Changed Everything

Bruce Buffer's journey to becoming the "Voice of the Octagon" can be traced back to a chance meeting that forever altered the course of his life. In the early 1990s, Bruce was working as a professional announcer for various events , including motocross and surfing competitions. It was during one such event that he crossed paths with someone who would prove instrumental in his UFC career.

At a motocross event, Bruce Buffer was approached by an attendee who happened to be friends with Rorion Gracie, one of the co-founders of the UFC. Intrigued by Bruce's announcing skills, this connection led to an introduction to the UFC's inner circle.

UFC Debut and Rising Stardom

Bruce Buffer made his UFC debut at UFC 8, which took place on February 16, 1996. His initial salary for that event was a mere $1,000. Little did he know that this was the beginning of an incredible journey.

As the UFC continued to grow in popularity, so did Bruce Buffer's stature as its official ring announcer. His distinctive style, charisma, and showmanship became a defining aspect of the UFC's presentation. Fans eagerly anticipated his spirited introductions, and fighters respected his professionalism and enthusiasm.

Building a Legacy

Over the years, Bruce Buffer's fame transcended the Octagon. His catchphrase, "It's time!" became synonymous with the excitement of UFC events. He introduced countless legendary fighters and played a crucial role in making each fight night a memorable spectacle.

Beyond his work in the Octagon, Bruce Buffer became a respected figure in the world of sports and entertainment. He appeared in movies, television shows, and even video games. His influence extended far beyond announcing, making him one of the most recognizable figures associated with the UFC.

Bruce Buffer's journey from a young announcer with a passion for entertainment to the iconic "Voice of the Octagon" is a testament to his unwavering dedication and unmistakable talent. His unique style and unforgettable catchphrase have left an indelible mark on the world of mixed martial arts. Today, Bruce Buffer remains an integral part of the UFC, adding an extra layer of excitement to every fight night and ensuring that the UFC experience is one that fans will never forget.

Chapter 24: The Crucial Role of Mouthguards in Fighter Safety

Mouthguards are often regarded as one of the unsung heroes of the UFC, silently protecting fighters from potentially devastating injuries. In the world of mixed martial arts (MMA), where powerful strikes and grappling maneuvers are the norm, the importance of mouthguards cannot be overstated.

The Anatomy of a Mouthguard

At first glance, a mouthguard might seem like a simple piece of equipment. It's a moldable, rubbery device that fits over a fighter's teeth, right? While that's a basic description, the real magic happens when a fighter clenches down on it. Mouthguards are designed to be a shock-absorbing barrier between a fighter's upper and lower jaws.

Preventing Dental Disaster

One of the most obvious roles of a mouthguard is to protect a fighter's teeth. In the heat of battle, with fists, elbows, and knees flying, there's a significant risk of dental injury. A solid punch to the jaw without a mouthguard could easily result in chipped or broken teeth. While dental repairs are possible, they can be costly and painful. Mouthguards serve as the first line of defense against this kind of dental disaster.

Stabilizing the Jaw

Beyond dental protection, mouthguards also play a crucial role in stabilizing the jaw. The jaw joint (temporomandibular joint or TMJ) is a complex hinge that can be vulnerable to dislocations or fractures, especially during intense grappling exchanges. A well-fitted mouthguard helps hold the jaw in place, reducing the risk of these types of injuries.

Mitigating the Risk of Concussions

It might not be immediately obvious, but mouthguards can indirectly contribute to reducing the risk of concussions. When a fighter takes a strike to the head, the force is partially absorbed by the mouthguard. While the primary purpose of the mouthguard is to protect the teeth and jaw, it also helps disperse some of the impact force, potentially lessening the severity of head trauma.

Custom-Fitted for Optimal Protection

Fighters in the UFC have access to some of the best equipment and resources in the sport, including custom-fitted mouthguards. These mouthguards are precisely molded to the fighter's teeth and jaw, ensuring a snug fit and maximum protection. Custom mouthguards provide a level of comfort and security that can make a significant difference during a fight.

Regulations and Fighter Responsibility

UFC regulations mandate that fighters wear mouthguards during their bouts. It's not just a suggestion; it's a critical safety requirement. Fighters are responsible for ensuring they have a properly fitted mouthguard that meets the UFC's safety standards. This includes checking the mouthguard's condition before each fight to ensure it can provide the necessary protection.

In the high-stakes world of MMA, where the difference between victory and defeat can be a split second, every piece of safety equipment plays a vital role. Mouthguards are the unsung heroes, quietly doing their job to protect fighters' teeth, jaws, and overall well-being.

Chapter 25: Honoring Legends - The UFC Hall of Fame

In the world of mixed martial arts (MMA), where fighters often showcase incredible courage, skill, and heart, the UFC Hall of Fame stands as a testament to the sport's most exceptional individuals. Established in 2003, this hallowed institution pays tribute to legendary fighters, coaches, and other significant contributors who have left an indelible mark on the Ultimate Fighting Championship.

A Place of Legends

The UFC Hall of Fame is not a physical building like many traditional sports halls of fame. Instead, it's a virtual institution that exists to honor those who have made extraordinary contributions to the sport. Fighters inducted into the Hall of Fame are recognized for their exceptional careers, memorable moments, and the impact they've had on the world of MMA.

Induction Categories

Over the years, the UFC has introduced various categories for induction into its Hall of Fame, ensuring that fighters, coaches, and other contributors receive the recognition they deserve. These categories include:

Modern Era Wing: This category honors fighters who have made significant contributions to the sport during the modern era of MMA, roughly from the early 1990s onwards.

Pioneer Era Wing: For fighters who competed during the formative years of MMA, when rules and regulations were still evolving.

Contributors: This category acknowledges individuals who have made a substantial impact on the UFC in roles other than fighting, such as coaches, officials, or executives.

Fight Wing: Reserved for fights that are considered iconic moments in the history of the sport.

Legends Immortalized

Numerous legendary fighters have been inducted into the UFC Hall of Fame. Names like Chuck Liddell, Randy Couture, Royce Gracie, and Anderson Silva adorn its virtual halls. These fighters are celebrated not only for their achievements inside the Octagon but also for the inspiration they've provided to countless fans and aspiring fighters.

Iconic Moments in the Fight Wing

In addition to individual fighters and contributors, the UFC Hall of Fame also recognizes extraordinary fights that have left a lasting impression on fans. These fights are often characterized by their incredible action, dramatic twists and turns, and their significance in shaping the sport's history. Each fight enshrined in the

Fight Wing represents a unique chapter in the story of MMA.

The Ultimate Recognition

Being inducted into the UFC Hall of Fame is the ultimate recognition of a fighter's or contributor's impact on the sport. It's an acknowledgment that their legacy extends far beyond their time in the cage. These individuals have not only achieved greatness but have also helped elevate the sport of MMA to new heights.

Continuing to Honor Excellence

As the UFC continues to grow and evolve, the Hall of Fame serves as a reminder of the sport's rich history and the individuals who have played a pivotal role in shaping its future. With each new generation of fighters and contributors, the Hall of Fame continues to expand, ensuring that the legacy of MMA lives on and that those who've left an indelible mark are forever honored.

Chapter 26: Hand Wrapping in the UFC

Hand wrapping is a critical aspect of a fighter's preparation in the UFC. Before stepping into the Octagon, fighters go through a meticulous process of wrapping their hands to provide essential support and protection to their wrists and knuckles. This process ensures their hands can withstand the tremendous impact that comes with striking and grappling during a fight.

The Importance of Hand Wrapping

Hand wrapping is not just a formality; it's a crucial safety measure that helps prevent hand and wrist injuries during a fight. The force generated during punches and strikes can lead to broken bones, sprained wrists, and dislocated knuckles if a fighter's hands aren't adequately protected. Hand wraps act as a supportive layer between the fighter's skin and the boxing gloves, absorbing the shock and minimizing the risk of injuries.

The Process of Hand Wrapping

The hand wrapping process is highly regulated by the UFC to ensure fairness and safety for all fighters. While each fighter may have specific preferences for how their hands are wrapped, there are specific rules and guidelines that all fighters must follow.

Materials: The most commonly used material for hand wraps is a combination of cloth and gauze. This blend provides flexibility and support while conforming to the shape of the fighter's hand.

Length: Hand wraps are typically around 180 inches long, which allows for adequate coverage and support.

Padding: To protect the knuckles and wrists, fighters often place extra padding over these areas. Some fighters prefer extra padding for their thumb as well.

Technique: The process of wrapping hands is intricate and can vary from fighter to fighter. It involves meticulously winding the cloth around the hand, fingers, and wrist to create a secure and supportive structure.

Tape: Once the hand wraps are in place, tape is used to secure the wraps and keep them from unraveling during the fight.

Fighter Preferences

Fighters often have unique preferences when it comes to hand wrapping. Some may prefer a tighter wrap for added support, while others opt for a looser wrap to allow for greater flexibility. Additionally, fighters may choose different types of tape and padding to cater to their individual needs.

Hand Wrapping Controversies

Over the years, there have been controversies in combat sports regarding hand wrapping. Some fighters have been accused of tampering with their hand wraps to gain an unfair advantage. In response, organizations like the UFC have implemented strict regulations and even introduced pre-fight checks to ensure that fighters adhere to the rules.

Injury Prevention

Hand wrapping is a fundamental part of injury prevention in the UFC. By providing crucial support to the hands, wrists, and knuckles, fighters can unleash their striking power and grappling techniques with confidence, knowing that their hands are protected. This not only ensures the fighter's safety but also contributes to the overall integrity and competitiveness of the sport.

Hand wrapping in the UFC is a vital practice that prioritizes fighter safety and injury prevention. It allows fighters to perform at their best while minimizing the risk of hand and wrist injuries during bouts. The process is highly regulated to maintain fairness and uphold the principles of sportsmanship in the Octagon.

Chapter 27: Scoring System in the UFC

In the earlier days of the UFC, determining the winner of a fight was often subjective and sometimes led to controversial decisions. However, with the growth and professionalization of the sport, the UFC implemented a standardized scoring system to provide clarity and consistency in determining the victor of each contest.

The 10-Point Must System

The scoring system used in the UFC is known as the 10-Point Must System. This system, widely adopted in combat sports, is straightforward in principle. At the end of each round, three judges evaluate the performance of the fighters and assign a score to each based on their performance during the round.

> **Winner of the Round:** The fighter deemed to have won the round is awarded ten points.
>
> **Loser of the Round:** The opponent, if they performed competitively but didn't win the round, typically receives nine points.
>
> **Point Deductions:** If a fighter commits fouls or violates the rules, the judges can deduct one or more points from their score for that round.
>
> **Dominance:** In cases where one fighter significantly outperforms the other, the winning fighter might be awarded 10-8 or even 10-7 in rare instances.

Judging Criteria

The judges use specific criteria to evaluate a fighter's performance during each round:

Effective Striking and Grappling: Judges assess the quality and effectiveness of a fighter's striking and grappling techniques. Clean, impactful strikes, successful takedowns, and submission attempts are all factors that contribute to a higher score.

Octagon Control: Fighters who dictate the pace of the fight, control the center of the Octagon, and push the action are typically favored by judges.

Effective Aggression: Judges look for fighters who press the action and maintain forward momentum without recklessness. Effective aggression is an essential element in scoring.

Defense: A fighter's ability to defend against strikes, takedowns, and submission attempts is also considered. Effective defense can sway judges in a fighter's favor, especially if they are facing a relentless opponent.

Damage: Visible damage inflicted on an opponent, such as cuts, swelling, or knockdowns, can influence judges' scores.

Role of Judges and Referee

Three judges seated cage-side are responsible for evaluating the fight. They observe the action, score each round, and communicate their scores to the overseeing commission. The referee is responsible for enforcing the rules, ensuring fighter safety, and making decisions regarding stoppages.

Scoring Controversies

Despite the implementation of the 10-Point Must System, scoring controversies still arise in the UFC. Some fights end in contentious decisions where fans, fighters, and analysts may disagree with the judges' assessments. These controversies are an inherent part of combat sports and continue to fuel discussions within the MMA community.

Remedies and Reforms

To address scoring controversies and promote transparency, the UFC and other MMA organizations have taken steps to improve judging. This includes providing additional training to judges, implementing instant replay for certain situations, and exploring alternative scoring systems.

The UFC's use of the 10-Point Must System has brought consistency and structure to the scoring of fights, ensuring that winners are determined based on their performance in each round. While controversies persist, the promotion remains committed to refining the judging process and promoting fairness in the Octagon.

Chapter 28: The Sanitization Ritual of the Octagon

The Octagon, the iconic battleground of the UFC, is not just a symbol of combat; it's a place where athletes put their skills and bodies to the test. The safety and well-being of fighters are paramount, and one aspect that underscores this commitment is the meticulous sanitization of the Octagon between fights.

Fighter Safety and Sanitization

The importance of sanitization in the Octagon cannot be overstated, especially in the context of combat sports. Fighters come into direct contact with the canvas, which can be exposed to sweat, blood, saliva, and other bodily fluids during a fight. To mitigate the risk of infection and ensure a safe environment for fighters, the UFC has implemented strict sanitization protocols.

Immediate Post-Fight Sanitization

As soon as a fight concludes and the fighters exit the Octagon, a team of professionals springs into action. They wear gloves and utilize cleaning agents specifically designed to disinfect and sanitize surfaces. These professionals pay meticulous attention to detail, ensuring that every inch of the Octagon is thoroughly cleaned.

The Cleaning Process

1. **Canvas Sanitization:** The canvas, where the majority of the action takes place, is cleaned meticulously. Cleaning agents are applied to remove any visible residue, and disinfectants are used to eliminate bacteria and pathogens. This step ensures that the surface is safe for the next set of fighters.
2. **Corner Stools and Equipment:** Fighter corners often bring stools, water bottles, and other equipment into the Octagon. These items are also subjected to sanitization to prevent cross-contamination.
3. **Safety for Officials:** Referees and other officials involved in the fight are also protected. Sanitization protocols extend to their uniforms and equipment, minimizing the risk of any potential health hazards.
4. **Cage Panels:** The cage itself is not neglected. The metal structure is cleaned and inspected for any potential hazards, ensuring that it remains in optimal condition.

Biohazard Management

Given the nature of combat sports, the UFC is well-prepared to handle biohazardous materials. Blood and other bodily fluids are treated with extreme caution. The removal of these substances follows strict safety procedures, protecting all personnel involved in the cleaning process.

Health and Safety Protocols

In addition to fight-specific sanitization, the UFC maintains stringent health and safety protocols throughout events. Fighters undergo medical examinations before and after fights, and there are medical personnel on-site to respond to any injuries or health concerns. These measures are part of the organization's commitment to ensuring fighter well-being.

COVID-19 Pandemic Considerations

The COVID-19 pandemic brought additional challenges to event sanitization. The UFC responded by implementing comprehensive health and safety protocols, including regular testing, quarantine measures, and strict adherence to public health guidelines. The organization's commitment to fighter safety remained unwavering, even in the face of the global health crisis.

The UFC's rigorous sanitization rituals between fights serve as a testament to the organization's dedication to fighter safety. These protocols not only maintain a clean and safe environment but also contribute to the overall integrity and professionalism of the sport.

Chapter 29: The Fighter's Crucible: Pre-Bout Medical Examinations

In the electrifying world of the UFC, fighters step into the Octagon with determination, skill, and unparalleled combat prowess. However, before they engage in battle, every fighter must undergo rigorous medical examinations. These examinations are a crucial aspect of ensuring fighter safety and the integrity of the sport.

A Non-Negotiable Requirement

Medical examinations for UFC fighters are not optional; they are mandatory and non-negotiable. This means that no fighter is allowed to compete unless they pass the required medical tests, ensuring that they are physically fit and healthy enough to step into the Octagon.

The Pre-Fight Medical Checklist

1. **Physical Examination:** The process begins with a comprehensive physical examination conducted by a licensed medical professional. This examination evaluates a fighter's overall health and identifies any pre-existing conditions that might affect their ability to compete safely.
2. **Neurological Assessment:** Neurological health is of paramount importance in combat sports. Fighters are subjected to a battery of neurological tests, which may include

assessments of reflexes, coordination, and cognitive function. These tests aim to detect any signs of concussions or other neurological issues.
3. **Cardiovascular Evaluation:** The cardiovascular system is put under scrutiny to ensure that fighters can endure the physical demands of a bout. Tests may include EKGs, stress tests, and blood pressure monitoring.
4. **Blood Work:** Fighters undergo a series of blood tests to check for infectious diseases, blood disorders, and performance-enhancing substances. These tests help maintain fairness and safety within the sport.
5. **Eye Examination:** Vision is critical in combat sports. Fighters' eyesight is evaluated to ensure they have optimal vision and can react effectively to their opponent's movements.
6. **Dental Examination:** Dental health might seem unrelated, but it's crucial in a sport where impacts to the face are common. Fighters must have dental evaluations to address any issues that could worsen during a bout.
7. **Weight Check:** While not strictly a medical examination, fighters must also undergo weight checks. Weight cutting is a common practice in combat sports, and fighters must meet the weight limit for their respective weight class. If they fail to do so, they may be disqualified or forced to compete in a different division.

The Role of Medical Professionals

Medical professionals, including physicians, neurologists, cardiologists, and optometrists, play a vital role in ensuring the health and safety of fighters. They bring their expertise to the table, carefully assessing fighters and providing recommendations based on their findings. In some cases, fighters may require further evaluation or treatment before they are cleared to compete.

Fighter Safety and Integrity

The UFC's commitment to fighter safety and the integrity of the sport is evident in the stringent pre-fight medical examinations. These measures not only protect the fighters but also uphold the reputation of mixed martial arts as a legitimate and professional sport.

The Human Element

While medical examinations are thorough and scientifically grounded, there is also a human element involved. Fighters' careers, dreams, and livelihoods are at stake. Medical professionals must make tough calls, and fighters may be disappointed if they are not cleared to compete. Nevertheless, this is a testament to the UFC's unwavering dedication to safety.

Pre-fight medical examinations are a cornerstone of the UFC's commitment to fighter well-being and the credibility of the sport. These examinations ensure that fighters enter the Octagon in the best possible physical condition, ready to showcase their skills and entertain fans around the world.

Chapter 30: The Art and Peril of Weight Cutting in the UFC

In the high-stakes world of mixed martial arts (MMA), fighters often embark on a perilous journey in the days leading up to a bout - a journey known as weight cutting. This practice, while common, is a complex and sometimes dangerous aspect of the sport.

The Weight Class System

The UFC, like many combat sports, employs a weight class system. Fighters are divided into specific weight categories, ranging from flyweight to heavyweight. Competing in a designated weight class ensures a level playing field, as fighters of similar sizes and weights face off against each other.

The Need to Cut Weight

Many fighters walk around above their designated weight class in their everyday lives. To compete at a lower weight class, they must lose a significant amount of weight during the days leading up to the weigh-in. This practice is known as "weight cutting."

The Process of Weight Cutting

Weight cutting involves a multifaceted approach, and fighters employ various methods to shed excess pounds:

1. **Dehydration:** The most common method is water manipulation. Fighters reduce their fluid intake and employ techniques like hot baths, saunas, and sweat suits to sweat out excess water weight. This can lead to severe dehydration, which poses significant health risks.
2. **Dietary Restrictions:** Fighters adhere to strict diets in the weeks leading up to the fight. They limit their calorie intake and consume foods that promote weight loss. This can lead to malnutrition and decreased energy levels.
3. **Exercise:** Fighters increase their training intensity to burn calories and shed pounds. This intense training can lead to physical exhaustion and increased injury risk.
4. **Safer Methods:** Some fighters use more controlled methods, such as gradual weight loss through diet and exercise, to avoid extreme measures. However, this approach may still involve significant weight loss.

The Weigh-In Ritual

The culmination of the weight cutting process is the official weigh-in, which takes place the day before the fight. Fighters must meet the weight limit for their designated class. The weigh-in is a highly anticipated event, often attended by fans and media, and it sets the stage for the fight.

Health Risks and Controversies

Weight cutting is not without its dangers. Severe dehydration can lead to kidney damage, heat stroke, and other life-threatening conditions. Fighters have occasionally suffered health crises during weight cuts, raising concerns about the practice.

The UFC and other MMA organizations have taken steps to address these issues. They've introduced early weigh-ins to give fighters more time to rehydrate and recover. Additionally, some have explored the possibility of introducing additional weight classes to reduce the incentive for extreme weight cutting.

Weight cutting is a complex and controversial practice in the world of MMA, one that balances the need for competitive fairness with the health and safety of the fighters. It remains a topic of debate within the sport, as stakeholders seek solutions to mitigate its risks while preserving the integrity of the weight class system.

Chapter 31: Official UFC Fighter Rankings

In the ever-evolving landscape of mixed martial arts, where fighters constantly seek to prove their worth inside the Octagon, the UFC introduced official fighter rankings to provide structure and clarity to the competitive field. These rankings serve as a vital tool for fans, fighters, and the organization itself, guiding matchmaking decisions, title shot opportunities, and the overall narrative of the sport.

The Birth of Fighter Rankings

Before the introduction of official rankings, determining the hierarchy of fighters in each weight class was often a matter of personal opinions, fan debates, and promotional narratives. Fighters' records and recent performances played a significant role in matchmaking, but there was no objective system in place to assess their standing accurately.

In February 2013, the UFC unveiled its first official fighter rankings, which covered eight of the promotion's weight divisions. The rankings aimed to provide transparency and objectivity in determining fighters' positions based on their recent performances, records, and other factors such as quality of opposition.

The Methodology

The official UFC fighter rankings are compiled by a panel of selected media members from various reputable outlets who cover the sport extensively. This panel is chosen by the UFC and is made up of journalists, analysts, and reporters who have demonstrated their knowledge of MMA.

The ranking process involves panel members submitting their individual rankings for each weight division. These submissions are then aggregated, and a consensus ranking is created for each fighter in the division. The fighters are ranked from 1 to 15, with the champion holding the top spot, followed by the top contenders.

Several criteria come into play when panel members cast their votes:

1. **Recent Performance:** Fighters' recent wins and losses weigh heavily in the rankings. Victories over higher-ranked opponents can significantly boost a fighter's standing.
2. **Quality of Opposition:** The caliber of opponents a fighter faces also matters. Beating well-regarded opponents carries more weight than victories over lower-ranked fighters.
3. **Consistency:** Fighters who consistently perform well over time are likely to maintain or improve their rankings.
4. **Dominance:** Fighters who finish their opponents impressively, whether by knockout or submission, may receive a higher ranking.

5. **Title Holders:** Champions automatically occupy the top spot in their respective divisions.

The Impact of Rankings

Official UFC fighter rankings have had several important impacts on the sport:

1. **Matchmaking:** Rankings provide a foundation for matchmaking decisions. Fighters ranked near the top of their division are often matched against each other, leading to high-stakes contests and clear pathways to title shots.
2. **Title Shot Opportunities:** The rankings play a crucial role in determining which fighters earn title shot opportunities. Typically, a fighter must be ranked highly or have an impressive winning streak to challenge for a championship.
3. **Fan Engagement:** Rankings offer fans a clear understanding of where their favorite fighters stand in the division. This transparency sparks discussions and debates among fans and analysts.
4. **Fighter Motivation:** For fighters, climbing the rankings is a clear path to championship glory and financial rewards. Rankings provide a tangible goal for fighters to pursue.
5. **Media and Promotion:** The UFC and other MMA media outlets frequently reference the official rankings in promotional materials, press releases, and broadcasts, adding legitimacy to the sport.

6. **Criticisms and Controversies**
7. Despite their benefits, the official UFC fighter rankings have not been without controversy. Some criticisms include:
8. **Lack of Transparency:** The methodology behind the rankings is not made public. Critics argue that more transparency in the process could improve its credibility.
9. **Panel Selection:** The selection of panel members has been a subject of debate, with some questioning the qualifications and potential biases of certain individuals.
10. **Inactivity:** Fighters who are inactive due to injuries or contract disputes can maintain their rankings, which some argue can lead to stagnation in the divisions.
11. **Subjectivity:** While the rankings aim for objectivity, there is still a level of subjectivity involved in panel members' assessments.
12. **Discrepancies:** From time to time, there are discrepancies in the rankings that lead to debate and controversy within the MMA community.

The official UFC fighter rankings have become an integral part of the sport, providing structure and clarity in a dynamic and ever-changing landscape. While they have faced their share of criticisms and controversies, they continue to play a significant role in guiding the trajectory of fighters' careers and shaping the narratives of the UFC's various weight divisions. These rankings are a testament to the sport's evolution and its commitment to professionalism and transparency.

Chapter 32: PRIME Drinks and the UFC

PRIME is a company known for its unique line of enhanced water beverages designed to support hydration and recovery. These drinks are formulated with a blend of electrolytes, antioxidants, and other essential nutrients. PRIME's mission aligns perfectly with the demands of UFC fighters, who require the utmost in physical conditioning, hydration, and recovery.

A Strategic Partnership

The partnership between PRIME and the UFC was a strategic move for both parties. It provided PRIME with a high-profile platform to showcase its products to a diverse and dedicated fan base, while the UFC gained a valuable sponsor known for its commitment to health and performance.

Official Hydration Partner

PRIME's involvement with the UFC extended beyond branding and promotion. They became the "Official Hydration Partner" of the UFC, which meant that PRIME drinks were readily available to fighters and staff during fight week and events. This partnership was a significant step for the UFC in ensuring the optimal health and performance of its athletes.

Hydration and MMA

Hydration is a crucial aspect of MMA training and competition. Fighters need to maintain their energy levels, focus, and overall health throughout their grueling training sessions and fights. Dehydration can lead to decreased performance, increased risk of injury, and even hospitalization.

Tailored to Fighter Needs

PRIME drinks provided a solution tailored to the specific needs of fighters. They offered a convenient and effective way for fighters to stay properly hydrated during their weight cuts, training sessions, and, most importantly, during their fights in the Octagon.

Promoting Fighter Well-Being

The presence of PRIME drinks in the UFC also sent a powerful message about the importance of proper hydration in combat sports. It highlighted the UFC's commitment to the well-being of its athletes and set a standard for other organizations in the world of MMA to follow.

The partnership between the UFC and PRIME drinks was a significant development in the world of mixed martial arts. It not only provided fighters with a valuable resource for hydration and recovery but also emphasized the importance of fighter health and safety in the sport. As the UFC continues to evolve and grow, such partnerships will likely play an increasingly crucial role in supporting fighters and promoting their well-being.

Chapter 33: Bruce Lee's Influence on the UFC

Bruce Lee is undoubtedly one of the most iconic figures in martial arts history. His philosophy, fighting style, and approach to combat have left an indelible mark on the world. Often credited as the father of modern mixed martial arts (MMA), Bruce Lee's influence on the creation and development of the UFC is profound.

Jeet Kune Do: The Art of Simplicity

At the heart of Bruce Lee's martial arts philosophy was the concept of Jeet Kune Do, which translates to "The Way of the Intercepting Fist." Lee believed in the idea of practicality and simplicity in combat. He encouraged martial artists to absorb what was useful from various styles and discard what was not, constantly evolving and adapting.

Bruce Lee's Impact on Fighters

Many fighters who later became part of the UFC's early history were deeply influenced by Bruce Lee's philosophy. They admired his commitment to breaking down traditional barriers in martial arts and his emphasis on adaptability, speed, and fluidity in combat.

Enter the Dragon: Bruce Lee's Films

Bruce Lee's movies, particularly "Enter the Dragon," introduced martial arts to a global audience. His exceptional martial skills, charisma, and philosophy made him a cultural icon and inspired countless individuals to explore martial arts.

The UFC's Beginnings

The UFC was founded in 1993, and its initial concept drew inspiration from Bruce Lee's ideas. The idea was to create a platform where fighters from different martial arts disciplines could test their skills against one another. The early UFC events featured a wide range of martial artists, including boxers, wrestlers, karate practitioners, and more.

No Rules, No Weight Classes

In its early days, the UFC had minimal rules and no weight classes, mirroring Bruce Lee's belief that fighting should be practical and adaptable. These early events were often billed as "no holds barred" contests, where almost anything was allowed.

Bruce Lee's Philosophy in Action

The spirit of Jeet Kune Do, as espoused by Bruce Lee, found its way into the Octagon. Fighters were encouraged to adopt a well-rounded approach to combat, incorporating techniques from various martial arts disciplines. This diversity of skills became a hallmark of the UFC.

The Evolution of MMA

As the UFC evolved, so did the sport of MMA. Bruce Lee's philosophy served as a foundation upon which the UFC and MMA built their principles. The sport gradually introduced weight classes, added rules for fighter safety, and developed into a global phenomenon.

Bruce Lee's Legacy

Bruce Lee's influence on the UFC is a testament to the enduring impact of his philosophy. He inspired a generation of fighters to challenge conventions, to seek knowledge from various sources, and to constantly adapt and evolve in their pursuit of martial excellence.

In the end, the UFC stands as a living embodiment of Bruce Lee's core principles: adaptability, practicality, and the quest for the most effective martial arts techniques. As MMA continues to grow and develop, Bruce Lee's legacy remains an integral part of its DNA, inspiring fighters to strive for greatness both inside and outside the Octagon.

Chapter 34: The UFC Video Game Series

In the world of sports video games, few titles capture the essence of mixed martial arts (MMA) quite like the UFC video game series. Developed by EA Sports and published by Electronic Arts, these games allow fans to step into the virtual Octagon and experience the intensity, strategy, and excitement of UFC fights from the comfort of their own living rooms.

A Brief History

The journey of the UFC video game series began with the release of "UFC: Tapout" in 2002 for the original Xbox console. However, it wasn't until 2009 that the franchise truly gained traction with the launch of "UFC 2009 Undisputed." This marked the start of a long and successful partnership between the UFC and video game developers.

The Undisputed Era

"UFC 2009 Undisputed" introduced fans to a new level of realism in MMA gaming. With a roster of over 80 fighters, realistic fighting mechanics, and a career mode where players could create and manage their fighters, the game was an instant hit.

This success was followed by "UFC Undisputed 2010" and "UFC Undisputed 3," both of which improved upon their predecessors with enhanced graphics, gameplay, and features. These titles allowed players to experience the evolution of MMA as they progressed through the years and took on legendary fighters.

The EA Era

In 2014, Electronic Arts acquired the exclusive rights to produce UFC video games, leading to the "EA Sports UFC" series. The first installment, "EA Sports UFC," was released in June 2014 for PlayStation 4 and Xbox One. It introduced a new physics-based striking system and stunning character models that brought fighters to life like never before.

The series continued with "EA Sports UFC 2" and "EA Sports UFC 3," each building upon the foundation of the previous game. These titles added more fighters, enhanced career modes, and refined the gameplay to provide a comprehensive MMA gaming experience.

The Current Generation

As of the latest available information in 2021, the most recent entry in the series is "EA Sports UFC 4." Released in August 2020, this game features a vast roster of fighters, improved striking and grappling mechanics, and an immersive career mode where players can rise through the ranks to become UFC champions.

Gameplay and Realism

The UFC video game series strives for realism in every aspect of gameplay. From the way fighters move and strike to the intricacies of ground and submission battles, the games provide an authentic representation of MMA combat. This attention to detail appeals not only to gamers but also to MMA enthusiasts who appreciate the sport's nuances.

Impact on UFC Fandom

The video game series has played a role in expanding the UFC's fan base. It introduces new fans to the sport and allows existing fans to engage with it in a unique way. Gamers can compete against friends or online opponents, test their skills in championship modes, and even recreate historic UFC matchups.

The Future of UFC Games

While the UFC video game series has already achieved a high level of realism and popularity, there's always room for improvement. Fans eagerly await future installments that may feature even more fighters, enhanced graphics, and innovative gameplay mechanics.

The UFC video game series has become an integral part of the MMA experience, allowing fans to immerse themselves in the world of the UFC and compete as their favorite fighters. Whether you're a dedicated gamer or a die-hard UFC fan, these games offer a thrilling way to step into the virtual Octagon and test your skills against the best fighters in the world.

Chapter 35: The Power of Walkout Songs

In the world of combat sports, the walkout song is more than just a tune to fill the arena; it's a powerful tool that fighters use to express themselves, pump up the crowd, and get into the right mindset before stepping into the Octagon. UFC fighters, like athletes in many other sports, often have signature walkout songs that become an integral part of their identity.

The Psychology of Music

Music has an incredible ability to influence our emotions and behaviors. It can motivate, calm, energize, and focus the mind. Understanding this power, fighters carefully select walkout songs to help them channel their emotions and enhance their performance. Whether it's the thundering beat of a heavy metal anthem or the soulful lyrics of a classic rock ballad, the right song can make a significant impact.

Personal Statements

A fighter's walkout song is a personal statement. It's a reflection of their personality, culture, and values. Some fighters choose songs that celebrate their heritage, while others opt for tracks that convey confidence, defiance, or even humor. These songs provide a glimpse into the fighter's inner world and can endear them to fans who resonate with their musical choices.

Iconic Walkouts

Over the years, certain fighters have become synonymous with their walkout songs. For example, Anderson Silva, the legendary former UFC Middleweight Champion, often walked out to the song "Ain't No Sunshine" by Bill Withers. This choice was both unexpected and iconic, serving as a perfect contrast to Silva's fierce fighting style.

Similarly, Conor McGregor, one of the most recognizable fighters in UFC history, often walked out to the tune of "The Foggy Dew" by Sinéad O'Connor and The Chieftains, celebrating his Irish heritage and electrifying the crowd.

Energizing the Arena

Walkout songs aren't just for the fighters; they're also for the fans. When a fighter's signature song begins to play, the arena erupts with excitement. Fans sing along, chant the fighter's name, and create an atmosphere that adds to the drama and spectacle of the event. It's a shared experience that unites the audience in support of their favorite fighters.

Mindset and Motivation

Fighters use their walkout songs to get into the right mental state. Many fighters describe the walkout as a surreal moment when they transition from the locker room's quiet focus to the explosive energy of the Octagon. The music serves as a bridge between these worlds, helping fighters shift their mindset from preparation to performance.

Evolution of Walkout Songs

Walkout songs have evolved over the years. In the early days of the UFC, fighters often walked out to generic arena rock tracks. However, as the sport gained popularity and fighters gained more control over their entrances, the music became more diverse and reflective of their individuality.

Today, fighters come out to an eclectic mix of genres, from hip-hop to country to heavy metal. Some even use custom-made walkout songs, adding an extra layer of personalization to their entrance.

The Fan's Perspective

For fans, walkout songs are an integral part of the UFC experience. They create emotional connections with fighters through shared musical tastes and lyrics that resonate with their own lives. When fans hear a fighter's walkout song outside of the Octagon, it often triggers memories of epic battles and triumphant moments.

The choice of a walkout song is a deeply personal decision for a fighter. It's a way for them to communicate with fans, psych themselves up, and create a memorable entrance. From iconic anthems to surprising selections, these songs have become an essential aspect of the UFC's rich tapestry, enhancing the spectacle and making every fight night feel like an unforgettable concert of combat.

Chapter 36: "The Ultimate Fighter" - Forging Champions on Reality TV

In the world of combat sports, few reality TV shows have had as significant an impact as "The Ultimate Fighter" (TUF). Premiering on January 17, 2005, TUF instantly became a game-changer for the UFC, offering fans a unique behind-the-scenes look at the journey to becoming a professional fighter.

The Birth of "The Ultimate Fighter"

The UFC's initial success was a mixed bag; while it attracted a dedicated fanbase, it was still struggling to break into the mainstream. The sport faced scrutiny, and some even labeled it as "human cockfighting." Something needed to change, and that change came in the form of a reality TV show.

The brainchild of UFC President Dana White and the production genius of Craig Piligian, "The Ultimate Fighter" was designed to give viewers an inside perspective on the lives, training, and struggles of aspiring fighters. It aimed to humanize the sport, allowing the audience to connect with the athletes on a personal level.

The First Season: A Game-Changer

The inaugural season of TUF featured light heavyweights and welterweights competing for a UFC contract. It pitted two of the UFC's most prominent fighters, Chuck Liddell and Randy Couture, against each other as coaches. This season showcased the grueling training, intense rivalries, and raw determination that goes into making a fighter.

The final bout between Forrest Griffin and Stephan Bonnar in the light heavyweight division is legendary in UFC history. The back-and-forth war was a rollercoaster of action that captivated fans and ultimately led to a UFC contract for both fighters. The fight was a turning point for the UFC, as it garnered record-breaking ratings and introduced the sport to a broader audience.

The Format

Each season of TUF typically features 16 fighters, divided into two teams, living and training together in a house for several weeks. These fighters compete in elimination-style tournaments, with the winners advancing to the finals. The coaches of each season are often established UFC fighters, adding an extra layer of drama to the show.

Notable Alumni

TUF has been a launchpad for many successful MMA careers. Fighters like Rashad Evans, Michael Bisping, Nate Diaz, and TJ Dillashaw all got their start on the show before going on to become UFC champions. TUF has consistently showcased the talent and potential of up-and-coming fighters, providing a platform for them to make a name for themselves.

Drama and Personalities

While the focus of TUF is on fighting, the reality TV format inevitably leads to drama and clashes of personalities. The confined living conditions, high-stress environment, and intense competition often result in memorable confrontations and rivalries. These interpersonal dynamics add an extra layer of intrigue to the show, making it a must-watch for fans.

Impact on the UFC

"The Ultimate Fighter" played a pivotal role in the UFC's rise to mainstream prominence. It helped break down misconceptions about the sport, created new fans, and built a bridge between fighters and the audience. The show's success led to a surge in the popularity of MMA and the UFC, and it remains an essential part of the promotion's legacy.

Evolution and Legacy

TUF has seen numerous seasons and adaptations, including international editions. While it has faced challenges and declining viewership in recent years, its impact on the sport and the UFC's growth cannot be overstated. It remains a valuable platform for discovering new talent and telling the stories of fighters striving for success in the Octagon.

"The Ultimate Fighter" isn't just a reality TV show; it's a significant chapter in the history of the UFC and mixed martial arts. It has given fans unforgettable moments, produced champions, and provided fighters with a pathway to achieving their dreams. TUF will forever be remembered as the show that helped make the UFC a global phenomenon.

Chapter 37: Tito Ortiz vs. Ken Shamrock - A Fierce UFC Rivalry

In the annals of UFC history, rivalries have been the lifeblood of the sport, captivating fans and elevating the stakes of each fight. Few rivalries have burned as intensely as the one between Tito Ortiz and Ken Shamrock, two MMA legends whose feud helped shape the early days of the UFC.

Tito Ortiz: The Young Lion

Tito Ortiz burst onto the MMA scene like a whirlwind. A former collegiate wrestler, Ortiz made his UFC debut at UFC 13 in 1997. With his brash personality and wrestling pedigree, he quickly became a fan favorite. His natural charisma and willingness to engage in trash talk made him a polarizing figure, drawing both ardent supporters and passionate detractors.

Ortiz's in-cage dominance matched his outsized personality. He was known for his ground-and-pound style and relentless pace, which often overwhelmed opponents. Ortiz's ascent in the light heavyweight division was rapid, and he eventually captured the UFC Light Heavyweight Championship.

Ken Shamrock: The Veteran Warrior

Ken Shamrock, on the other hand, was already a veteran of the fight game when Ortiz burst onto the scene. With a background in professional wrestling and a solid foundation in submission grappling, Shamrock was one of the early stars of MMA. His reputation as a submission specialist and his gritty fighting style endeared him to fans.

The clash of generations between Shamrock and Ortiz was evident. Shamrock was a seasoned warrior, while Ortiz represented the new breed of fighters entering the sport. This generational gap, coupled with Ortiz's brash trash talk, laid the foundation for their fierce rivalry.

The First Encounter: UFC 40

The rivalry between Ortiz and Shamrock reached its peak at UFC 40, where they faced off for the UFC Light Heavyweight Championship. The tension leading up to the fight was palpable, with Ortiz's provocative antics and Shamrock's stoic demeanor creating a perfect storm of drama.

When the two finally stepped into the Octagon, the world watched in anticipation. The fight was an intense battle, with Ortiz ultimately securing a TKO victory in the third round. While Ortiz emerged victorious, the rivalry was far from over.

Rematches and Feuds

The Ortiz vs. Shamrock rivalry didn't end with their first bout. In fact, it became a trilogy. They met again at UFC 61 in 2006, where Ortiz won by TKO. Despite the consecutive losses, Shamrock's indomitable spirit refused to let the rivalry fade away.

Their third and final fight took place at UFC 66 in December 2006. This time, Ortiz again emerged victorious, solidifying his dominance over Shamrock. However, the significance of their rivalry extended beyond the outcomes of their fights.

Legacy and Impact

The Ortiz vs. Shamrock rivalry played a pivotal role in the growth of the UFC during its formative years. Their heated exchanges, both verbal and physical, drew mainstream attention to the sport. Their trilogy of fights helped UFC events gain popularity, setting the stage for the organization's ascent into mainstream sports.

Beyond their rivalries and conflicts, both Ortiz and Shamrock contributed significantly to the sport of MMA. Ortiz, with his outspoken persona, became one of the UFC's most iconic figures. Shamrock, as a veteran fighter, helped establish MMA's legitimacy in its early days.

The rivalry between Tito Ortiz and Ken Shamrock was a defining chapter in the history of the UFC. It showcased the sport's evolution, the clash of generations, and the fierce determination of two warriors. While their battles inside the Octagon are now part of MMA lore, their impact on the growth of the UFC and MMA as a whole cannot be overstated.

Chapter 38: UFC 40 - "Vendetta" - A Pivotal Moment in MMA History

UFC 40, also known as "Vendetta," stands as a pivotal moment in the history of mixed martial arts (MMA). Held on November 22, 2002, at the MGM Grand Garden Arena in Las Vegas, Nevada, this event marked a turning point for the UFC and the sport as a whole.

A Struggling Promotion

Leading up to UFC 40, the Ultimate Fighting Championship was at a crossroads. The promotion was struggling financially and facing uncertainty about its future. Many states had banned MMA, and the sport faced criticism from politicians and regulatory bodies. It seemed like MMA's future was hanging in the balance.

The Tito Ortiz vs. Ken Shamrock Rivalry

One of the key elements that helped save the UFC from potential demise was the fierce rivalry between Tito Ortiz and Ken Shamrock, as mentioned in the previous chapter. The UFC capitalized on this heated feud, building anticipation for their matchup at UFC 40. The title fight between Ortiz and Shamrock served as the event's centerpiece and generated significant buzz.

The Ortiz vs. Shamrock Showdown

Tito Ortiz and Ken Shamrock headlined UFC 40 in a fight for the UFC Light Heavyweight Championship.

The anticipation for this bout was immense. Ortiz, the brash young champion, was determined to prove his dominance over Shamrock, the MMA legend. Shamrock, on the other hand, sought to turn the tide and capture the championship.

The fight itself was a thrilling contest. Ortiz and Shamrock engaged in a battle that went the distance, lasting for all five rounds. In the end, Ortiz was declared the winner by unanimous decision, solidifying his status as one of the sport's top fighters. While the result disappointed Shamrock's fans, the fight itself delivered on its promise of excitement and drama.

A Record-Breaking Night

UFC 40 was a financial and critical success. It shattered previous UFC pay-per-view records, drawing a massive audience. This surge in popularity was partly attributed to the Ortiz vs. Shamrock rivalry, but it also signaled a growing interest in MMA as a whole. The event garnered attention not only from hardcore fight fans but also from a wider audience.

The Ultimate Fighter Television Show

In addition to the Ortiz vs. Shamrock showdown, UFC 40 featured the debut of a new reality television series that would go on to play a significant role in the sport's growth: "The Ultimate Fighter" (TUF). This groundbreaking show provided up-and-coming fighters with a platform to showcase their skills and compete for a UFC contract. TUF would become a major factor in the UFC's resurgence.

Impact on MMA's Legitimacy

UFC 40's success marked a turning point for MMA's acceptance in the mainstream. It helped dispel some of the negative stereotypes associated with the sport and contributed to its growing legitimacy as a combat sport. With the popularity of "Vendetta," the UFC was on a path to overcoming adversity and solidifying its place in sports history.

UFC 40, "Vendetta," was a watershed moment in the sport of MMA. It showcased the power of compelling rivalries, the allure of high-stakes championship fights, and the potential for MMA to capture the imagination of a global audience. This event not only saved the UFC from financial turmoil but also paved the way for the sport's meteoric rise in the years to come.

Chapter 39: The Octagon Mat - A Custom Canvas for Combat

While the Octagon itself is an iconic symbol of the UFC, it's the canvas within that cage that sets the stage for every fight. The Octagon mat is more than just a surface for combat; it's a custom-made platform that holds significance for fighters and fans alike.

The Octagon Mat's Role

The Octagon mat serves multiple important functions during a UFC event. It provides a safe and controlled surface for fighters to compete on, minimizing the risk of injuries caused by uneven or slippery floors. Beyond its practical role, the mat also serves as a canvas for the sport's history, displaying the UFC logo, sponsors, and the name of the event.

Custom-Made for Each Event

One of the unique aspects of the Octagon mat is that it's custom-made for every UFC event. This attention to detail reflects the UFC's commitment to providing fighters and fans with a unique experience at each show.

The Design Process

The process of creating a custom Octagon mat begins well in advance of the event. It involves collaboration between the UFC's design team, sponsors, and the production crew. Here's an overview of the design process:

1. **Conceptualization:** The process starts with conceptualization, where the design team brainstorms ideas for the mat's appearance. This includes considering the event's theme, any special promotions, and sponsor logos.
2. **Sponsor Integration:** Sponsors play a significant role in MMA, and their logos are prominently featured on the mat. Integrating these logos into the design while maintaining a visually appealing look is a crucial part of the process.
3. **Graphics and Layout:** Once the design is finalized, the graphics and layout are created. This includes determining the placement of logos, the UFC logo, and any additional graphics or text.
4. **Quality and Durability:** The Octagon mat must be both visually impressive and durable. It undergoes rigorous testing to ensure it can withstand the demands of a UFC event. This includes testing for slip resistance and impact absorption.
5. **Printing and Production:** After final approval, the design is printed onto the mat's surface. This process requires specialized equipment to ensure high-quality, vibrant graphics.
6. **Installation:** On the day of the event, the custom Octagon mat is meticulously installed

inside the cage. It's an intricate process that requires precision to align the mat perfectly.

The Mat's Significance

For fighters, stepping onto the Octagon mat is a moment filled with emotion and anticipation. It's where they will test their skills, chase their dreams, and etch their names into MMA history. The Octagon mat is both the battleground and the canvas where their stories are written.

For fans, the mat is a familiar sight that signifies the start of a thrilling night of fights. It's where they witness incredible displays of athleticism, heart, and determination. The design of the mat often reflects the unique character of each event, from championship bouts to special occasions.

The Octagon mat may seem like a simple canvas, but it plays a significant role in the UFC's presentation of the sport. It's more than just a surface; it's a stage where fighters become legends and fans become witnesses to history. With each custom-made mat, the UFC continues to showcase its commitment to providing a unique and memorable experience for everyone involved in the world of MMA.

Chapter 40: Dana White - The Long Reign as UFC President

The Ultimate Fighting Championship, better known as the UFC, has seen significant growth and evolution since its inception in 1993. A pivotal figure in this journey has been Dana White, who has held the position of UFC President for many years. In this chapter, we delve into the remarkable tenure of Dana White and the profound impact he has had on the world of mixed martial arts (MMA).

The Early Days of Dana White

Dana White was born on July 28, 1969, in Manchester, Connecticut. Before his tenure as UFC President, White had a diverse career that included managing fighters, working in the boxing industry, and even serving as an aerobics instructor. His journey to becoming the face of the UFC began in the early 2000s when he was introduced to Lorenzo and Frank Fertitta, who would later purchase the UFC.

The Fertitta Brothers and the UFC Purchase

The Fertitta brothers, owners of Station Casinos, purchased the UFC for a mere $2 million in 2001. They recognized the potential of the sport and believed in its ability to grow. To help steer the ship, they brought in Dana White as the President.

The Turning Point: Zuffa Era

Under the Fertitta brothers' ownership and Dana White's leadership, the UFC underwent a significant transformation. White's passion, vision, and business acumen were instrumental in reshaping the UFC from a niche sport into a global phenomenon. Key milestones during his tenure include:

1. **Reform of Regulations**: White played a pivotal role in changing regulations to make the sport safer and more palatable to a wider audience. This included adopting weight classes, introducing rules, and implementing drug testing protocols.
2. **Expansion:** Dana White was instrumental in expanding the UFC's global reach. He promoted international talent and spearheaded efforts to host events in various countries, growing the UFC's fan base worldwide.
3. **The Ultimate Fighter:** The reality TV show "The Ultimate Fighter," co-created by Dana White, brought the sport and the UFC into the mainstream. The show not only produced stars but also captured the imagination of fans.
4. **Media Deals:** White was at the forefront of securing lucrative media deals that brought UFC content to millions of viewers, further establishing its presence in the sports world.
5. **Stars and Superfights:** He played a role in nurturing and promoting some of the biggest stars in MMA history, including Chuck Liddell, Randy Couture, Anderson Silva, Georges St-Pierre, Ronda Rousey, and Conor McGregor.

His efforts also led to historic crossover bouts like McGregor vs. Mayweather.

Challenges and Controversies

Dana White's tenure as UFC President hasn't been without challenges and controversies. Criticisms have arisen regarding fighter pay, negotiations, and fighter treatment. Nevertheless, White's unwavering commitment to the sport's growth has remained a driving force.

Dana White's Impact

Dana White's impact on the UFC is immeasurable. He transformed the organization from a fringe sport into a global powerhouse. His passion for the sport, promotional savvy, and tireless work ethic have made him a recognizable and respected figure in the world of combat sports.

The Future of Dana White and the UFC

As of my knowledge cutoff date in September 2021, Dana White continues to serve as the UFC President. His influence on the sport and the organization is likely to continue for years to come. However, it's important to note that circumstances may have changed since that time.

Dana White's journey from an aerobics instructor to the President of the UFC is a testament to his vision and dedication. His leadership has been instrumental in the growth of MMA, making the UFC a global phenomenon. While his tenure has not been without controversy, there's no denying the profound impact he has had on the sport and the organization.

Chapter 41: The UFC's Global Fan Base

The Ultimate Fighting Championship (UFC) has evolved from a small-scale, niche sport in the early '90s to a global phenomenon with a massive and diverse fan base. In this chapter, we'll explore how the UFC has garnered a worldwide following, transcending borders and cultures.

A Sport with Universal Appeal

Mixed martial arts (MMA) itself possesses qualities that resonate with people around the world. Unlike some traditional sports that may require specific equipment or facilities, MMA's raw and primal nature, along with its emphasis on individual skill and discipline, makes it accessible and captivating to a broad audience.

Global Expansion

One of the UFC's primary strategies for cultivating a global fan base has been international expansion. The organization has taken the Octagon to various corners of the world, hosting events on every inhabited continent except Antarctica. This expansion has not only introduced fans to live UFC action but has also given local fighters opportunities to compete on the biggest stage.

Local Talent and International Stars

A key element in the UFC's global appeal is its ability to create local heroes in different regions. While international stars like Conor McGregor and Anderson Silva draw fans worldwide, the promotion also actively seeks out and promotes talent from specific regions. For example, fighters like Khabib Nurmagomedov from Russia and Israel Adesanya from New Zealand have garnered massive followings in their home countries.

Broadcasting and Media Reach

The UFC's media strategy has played a crucial role in building its global fan base. The promotion has secured broadcasting deals with networks and streaming platforms in various countries, ensuring that fans worldwide can watch live events and follow the sport through highlight shows and documentaries.

Cultural Sensitivity and Adaptation

To succeed on the international stage, the UFC has made efforts to understand and adapt to local cultures and preferences. This includes considerations such as scheduling events to suit different time zones, respecting religious customs, and using marketing approaches that resonate with specific audiences.

Global Fan Engagement

The UFC recognizes the importance of engaging with its global fan base. The organization maintains an active presence on social media platforms, where fans from around the world can connect, share their passion for the sport, and interact with fighters. UFC events often feature fan-friendly experiences, such as meet-and-greets with fighters and fan festivals.

International Fighters and Cross-Cultural Exchanges

International fighters have played a crucial role in expanding the UFC's fan base. As fighters from different countries compete in the Octagon, they bring their unique styles and stories, attracting fans from their home regions and beyond. The UFC has also embraced cross-cultural exchanges, celebrating events like "International Fight Week," which showcases the diversity of the sport.

Challenges of Global Expansion

While the UFC's global expansion has been largely successful, it has not been without challenges. These include navigating different regulatory environments, overcoming language barriers, and addressing cultural sensitivities. The organization has had to adapt and learn from its experiences in various markets.

The Future of the UFC's Global Fan Base

As of my knowledge cutoff date in September 2021, the UFC's global fan base continued to grow. The organization's commitment to international expansion and fan engagement remained strong. However, the dynamics of the sports and entertainment industry are ever-evolving, and the UFC's strategies may have evolved since that time.

The UFC's global fan base is a testament to the universal appeal of mixed martial arts and the organization's relentless efforts to expand its reach. By showcasing international talent, adapting to local cultures, and engaging with fans worldwide, the UFC has become a truly global sporting phenomenon. Its ability to connect with people from diverse backgrounds and regions highlights the enduring power of combat sports to unite and entertain a worldwide audience.

Chapter 42: The Art of Cross-Training in MMA

Mixed martial arts is a unique combat sport that combines various fighting disciplines, such as boxing, wrestling, Brazilian Jiu-Jitsu (BJJ), Muay Thai, and more. To excel in this multifaceted sport, fighters often engage in cross-training, a practice that allows them to develop a wide range of skills and techniques. In this chapter, we will explore the significance of cross-training in MMA and how it has shaped the evolution of the sport.

The Versatility of MMA

MMA is often referred to as the "ultimate" or "complete" combat sport because it incorporates techniques and strategies from a multitude of martial arts disciplines. Unlike traditional combat sports with singular rule sets, MMA fighters must be proficient in various areas, both standing and on the ground. This versatility requires extensive training and cross-disciplinary skill development.

The Basics of Cross-Training

Cross-training is the practice of learning and integrating techniques from different martial arts disciplines into one's training regimen. MMA fighters typically cross-train in striking arts like boxing, kickboxing, and Muay Thai for stand-up combat and wrestling, BJJ, and judo for ground fighting. This multifaceted training approach helps fighters become well-rounded and adaptable in the cage.

Striking Arts: Boxing, Muay Thai, and Kickboxing

Many MMA fighters cross-train in striking arts to improve their punching, kicking, and clinching abilities. Boxing provides fighters with precise punching techniques, head movement, and footwork. Muay Thai adds powerful knee and elbow strikes, as well as a clinching game. Kickboxing combines punches and kicks seamlessly, promoting fluid transitions between striking techniques.

Grappling Arts: Wrestling and Brazilian Jiu-Jitsu

Wrestling is a foundational discipline in MMA, as it enables fighters to control their opponents, dictate positioning, and execute takedowns. Brazilian Jiu-Jitsu, with its focus on submissions and ground control, complements wrestling by providing fighters with a toolkit for submissions, sweeps, and escapes.

Combining Striking and Grappling

The key to successful cross-training is integrating striking and grappling seamlessly. MMA fighters develop their striking and grappling skills in tandem to ensure they can transition between ranges effectively. Sparring sessions often involve both striking and grappling, allowing fighters to practice these transitions under realistic conditions.

The Importance of Sparring Partners

Quality sparring partners are essential for cross-training. Fighters often seek out training camps or gyms with a diverse roster of training partners, each specializing in different martial arts. This variety allows fighters to adapt to different styles and techniques, preparing them for the unpredictability of MMA bouts.

The Evolution of MMA Skillsets

Over the years, the practice of cross-training has led to the evolution of MMA skillsets. Fighters are no longer limited to one specific style; instead, they develop hybrid fighting styles tailored to their strengths and preferences. The sport has witnessed a blending of techniques, resulting in innovations like "wrestling for MMA" and "MMA striking."

Strategic Adaptation

Fighters use cross-training to develop specific strategies for their opponents. For example, a fighter facing a dominant wrestler may focus on takedown defense and counter-wrestling. Alternatively, a striker facing a Brazilian Jiu-Jitsu black belt may emphasize keeping the fight standing and avoiding the ground.

Injuries and Longevity

While cross-training is invaluable for skill development, it can also be physically demanding. Fighters must manage their training intensity to prevent injuries and ensure their longevity in the sport. Proper conditioning and recovery techniques are essential aspects of a fighter's regimen.

Cross-training is the backbone of MMA skill development. Fighters who invest in learning various martial arts disciplines and integrating them seamlessly into their fighting style become formidable competitors in the Octagon. The evolution of MMA has been driven by fighters' abilities to cross-train, adapt, and continuously refine their techniques, making it one of the most dynamic and versatile combat sports in the world.

Chapter 43: The Enigmatic Striking Style of Anderson Silva

In the world of MMA, few fighters have achieved the level of striking excellence displayed by Anderson "The Spider" Silva. A true legend of the sport, Silva is celebrated not only for his victories but also for his unique and enigmatic striking style. In this chapter, we delve into the intricacies of Silva's striking prowess and the impact it has had on the sport.

The Emergence of a Striking Phenom

Anderson Silva, hailing from Brazil, burst onto the MMA scene with a striking style that was both unorthodox and mesmerizing. He was a striking prodigy, showcasing a mix of Muay Thai, traditional boxing, and the elusive capoeira, a Brazilian martial art known for its fluid, acrobatic movements. Silva's striking style quickly set him apart from his peers.

The Art of Precision Striking

Silva's striking style is characterized by precision and timing. He possesses an uncanny ability to gauge his opponent's movements and strike with surgical precision. His punches, kicks, and knee strikes find their mark with a level of accuracy that often leaves his opponents stunned and unable to defend effectively.

The Deadly Muay Thai Clinch

One of Silva's trademarks is his devastating clinch game, which borrows heavily from Muay Thai. His ability to control an opponent in the clinch and deliver devastating knee strikes to the body and head has led to some of the most iconic moments in MMA history. Silva's use of the clinch has often resulted in memorable knockouts.

Utilizing Unconventional Techniques

Silva is known for his creativity inside the cage. He has employed unconventional techniques like the front kick, often referred to as the "Silva stomp," to devastating effect. His use of such unexpected moves keeps opponents on edge, unsure of what to anticipate next.

Mind Games and Psychology

Silva's striking style extends beyond the physical realm. He is a master of psychological warfare, often taunting his opponents and luring them into making mistakes. His famous fight against Forrest Griffin, where he dodged strikes with casual ease, is a testament to his ability to mentally disrupt his adversaries.

Legendary Knockouts and Highlight Reels

Throughout his career, Silva compiled a highlight reel of incredible knockouts and striking displays. Fights against notable opponents like Rich Franklin, Vitor Belfort, and Chris Leben showcased his striking brilliance. These performances solidified his reputation as one of the greatest strikers in MMA history.

Influence on the Sport

Silva's unique striking style has left an indelible mark on the world of MMA. Many fighters have attempted to mimic his precision, adapt his techniques, or incorporate elements of his striking into their own arsenals. His influence can be seen in the evolution of striking techniques in the sport.

The Legacy of The Spider

Anderson Silva's striking style remains a source of fascination and admiration among MMA enthusiasts. His ability to seamlessly blend multiple striking disciplines, employ unconventional techniques, and manipulate opponents both physically and mentally has earned him a place in the pantheon of MMA legends. As we reflect on Silva's storied career, his striking artistry will forever be etched in the annals of combat sports history.

Chapter 44: The Diverse Spectrum of UFC Venue Sizes

One of the UFC's distinctive features is its ability to host events in a wide range of venues, from intimate arenas to colossal stadiums. This chapter explores how the UFC's adaptability in venue selection has contributed to its global success and the unique experiences it offers fans and fighters.

Small Arenas - The Birthplace of UFC

In the early days of the UFC, events were often held in small, intimate arenas. These venues, with limited seating capacities, provided an up-close and personal atmosphere for fans. The proximity to the Octagon allowed spectators to feel the raw intensity of the fights. These smaller arenas, including the McNichols Sports Arena in Denver, Colorado, where UFC 1 took place, played a pivotal role in the promotion's inception.

Casinos and Theatres - An Intimate Setting

As the UFC grew in popularity, it continued to hold events in more modest venues such as casinos and theatres. Locations like the Trump Taj Mahal in Atlantic City and the Joint at the Hard Rock Hotel & Casino in Las Vegas became synonymous with thrilling fights and packed houses. These venues provided a unique blend of entertainment, combining the excitement of casino gaming or the elegance of a theatre with the thrill of live combat sports.

Large Arenas - The UFC's Worldwide Expansion

The UFC's global expansion saw it step onto bigger stages, hosting events in large arenas. Locations like Madison Square Garden in New York City and the MGM Grand Garden Arena in Las Vegas became iconic venues for historic matchups. The larger seating capacities allowed more fans to witness the action live, making these events grand spectacles and unforgettable experiences.

Stadiums - Breaking Attendance Records

In an effort to set attendance records and reach broader audiences, the UFC ventured into massive stadiums. UFC 129 at the Rogers Centre in Toronto, Canada, for instance, drew over 55,000 fans, setting a North American MMA attendance record. Events in stadiums like the Etihad Stadium in Melbourne, Australia, and T-Mobile Arena in Las Vegas showcased the UFC's global appeal.

International Destinations - A World Tour

The UFC's willingness to host events in various countries has contributed to its global reach. From arenas in Brazil, Russia, and China to open-air stadiums in the United Arab Emirates, the promotion has taken MMA to diverse locations. These international ventures have not only thrilled local fans but also exposed the sport to new audiences worldwide.

Fight Island - A Unique Solution

Amid the COVID-19 pandemic, the UFC introduced "Fight Island" on Yas Island in Abu Dhabi. This custom-built venue allowed the organization to safely host events during travel restrictions. Fight Island featured a blend of open-air and arena-style venues, demonstrating the UFC's adaptability during challenging times.

A Venue for Every Occasion

The UFC's diverse selection of venues reflects its commitment to delivering unique experiences to fans and fighters alike. Whether it's the intimate setting of a small arena, the elegance of a theatre, the grandeur of a stadium, or the novelty of an international location, each venue offers a distinct atmosphere and memories that resonate with MMA enthusiasts. The UFC's ability to adapt to different venues has been a cornerstone of its global success, ensuring that there's a perfect stage for every UFC event.

Chapter 45: The Grand Spectacle of UFC Opening Ceremonies

UFC events aren't just about the fights inside the Octagon; they are also known for their elaborate and visually stunning opening ceremonies. These ceremonies are designed to captivate the audience, build anticipation, and pay tribute to the rich history and cultural significance of the sport of mixed martial arts.

The Walkout: A Fighter's Grand Entrance

The opening ceremonies typically begin with the walkout of the fighters. Each fighter's entrance is carefully choreographed, complete with dynamic lighting, music, and sometimes even pyrotechnics. The walkout is a moment for fighters to showcase their unique personalities and psych themselves up for the battle ahead.

National Anthems: A Show of Respect

Before the first fight begins, it's customary to perform the national anthems of both competing fighters. This gesture is a sign of respect for the diverse backgrounds and nationalities of the athletes. It's a reminder that the UFC is a global organization that brings together fighters from all corners of the world.

The UFC Signature Video

One of the most iconic elements of UFC opening ceremonies is the signature video. This video typically features highlights of the fighters on the card, dramatic music, and a powerful narration that sets the tone for the event. It serves as a powerful storytelling tool, building excitement and emotional connection with the fighters and the sport.

Special Performances: Celebrity Guests

Many UFC events feature special guest performers during the opening ceremony. These can include musical acts, celebrities, or even athletes from other sports. Their performances add an extra layer of entertainment to the event and often make for memorable moments.

The UFC Octagon Girls

The Octagon Girls play a significant role in the UFC opening ceremonies. They are not just there to look glamorous; they also hold up round cards to indicate which round is about to begin. Their presence adds to the visual spectacle of the event, and they are fan favorites.

Tributes and Homages: Remembering Legends

Sometimes, opening ceremonies include tributes and homages to legendary fighters or figures in the MMA world. These segments celebrate the history of the sport and pay respects to those who have made significant contributions.

The UFC President's Address

Before the first fight begins, UFC President Dana White often addresses the crowd. He sets the stage for the evening, expresses his excitement about the matchups, and thanks the fans for their support. His speeches are often met with cheers and applause.

The Unveiling of the Octagon

The climax of the opening ceremony is the unveiling of the Octagon. In a grand moment, the canvas is revealed, and the arena is transformed into the battleground for the evening. The Octagon is often bathed in dramatic lighting, further intensifying the anticipation.

The Prelude to Battle

The opening ceremony of a UFC event is more than just a prelude to the fights; it's an integral part of the overall experience. It's a time when fighters, fans, and the entire MMA community come together to celebrate the sport. These ceremonies are a testament to the UFC's commitment to delivering not only world-class fights but also a grand spectacle that leaves a lasting impression on everyone in attendance and watching around the world.

Chapter 46: Conor McGregor - The Notorious One

Conor McGregor, the Irish mixed martial artist, is not just a fighter; he's an icon in the world of combat sports. Known for his exceptional skills inside the Octagon and his larger-than-life personality outside of it, McGregor has earned the nickname "Notorious." In this chapter, we delve into the origins of this famous moniker and explore the man behind it.

The Birth of Notorious

Conor McGregor was born on July 14, 1988, in Crumlin, a suburb of Dublin, Ireland. His journey in combat sports began at a young age when he started training in boxing. As he honed his skills and transitioned into mixed martial arts (MMA), his brash and confident demeanor began to catch the attention of fans and media alike.

It was during his rise in the UFC that McGregor adopted the nickname "Notorious." The choice of the word "notorious" signifies his bold and sometimes controversial persona, both in and out of the cage. McGregor embraced the nickname as it perfectly encapsulated his unapologetic self-confidence and willingness to speak his mind.

A Remarkable UFC Career

McGregor made his UFC debut in April 2013 and quickly made a name for himself with his striking prowess and charisma. He became the first fighter in UFC history to hold titles in two weight classes simultaneously when he captured the Featherweight and Lightweight championships.

His accomplishments in the Octagon include notable victories over fighters like José Aldo, Dustin Poirier, and Eddie Alvarez. McGregor's fighting style is characterized by his precision striking, particularly his devastating left hand, which has earned him many knockout victories.

Not Just a Fighter: The McGregor Brand

What sets Conor McGregor apart is his ability to transcend the sport of MMA. He has effectively built a brand around himself, becoming a global sports and entertainment sensation. McGregor's confident and often brash demeanor, paired with his sharp wit, made him a polarizing figure that fans couldn't ignore.

Outside of fighting, McGregor has ventured into the world of business, launching his whiskey brand, Proper No. Twelve. He's also been involved in numerous high-profile promotional events and even took on boxing legend Floyd Mayweather in a crossover boxing match.

Challenges and Comebacks

While McGregor's career has been filled with triumphs, it has also been marked by setbacks and controversies.

He's faced legal issues, suspensions, and periods of inactivity. However, one constant in his career is his ability to rebound. McGregor has made successful comebacks, proving that he is a force to be reckoned with in the world of combat sports.

The Legacy of Notorious

Conor McGregor's impact on MMA cannot be overstated. He has drawn attention to the sport on a global scale and introduced many new fans to the world of UFC. His charismatic personality, combined with his incredible fighting talent, has solidified his status as one of the most iconic figures in combat sports history.

Notorious Forever

Conor McGregor's journey from a young fighter in Dublin to the global superstar known as "Notorious" is nothing short of remarkable. His impact on the sport of MMA and the world of entertainment is undeniable, and his legacy will continue to resonate for generations of fight fans. Whether loved or loathed, there's no denying that Conor McGregor is a name that will forever be synonymous with the UFC and the nickname "Notorious" will forever be etched in the annals of MMA history.

Chapter 47: The UFC's Worldwide Reach

The Ultimate Fighting Championship is not confined to a single corner of the globe. It's a global sporting phenomenon that has spread its octagonal cage to multiple continents. In this chapter, we'll explore the UFC's worldwide reach, showcasing its international expansion and the impact it has had on the sport of mixed martial arts (MMA).

The Early Days: U.S. Domination

The UFC was born in the United States in 1993, and initially, its events were primarily held within the country. The organization's first events took place in states like Colorado and Louisiana, and the Octagon was synonymous with American MMA.

Global Expansion Begins

As the sport gained traction and popularity, the UFC began to look beyond U.S. borders. In 1997, the UFC hosted its first event outside of the United States, in Yokohama, Japan. This marked the beginning of the organization's global expansion.

A New Millennium, a New Approach

The early 2000s saw the UFC's foray into international markets like the United Kingdom, Brazil, and Canada. The organization's "UFC: Brazil" series introduced Brazilian fighters to the world stage, and the "UFC:

United Kingdom" events were pivotal in popularizing MMA in Europe.

The Ultimate Fighter's Global Influence

The reality TV show, "The Ultimate Fighter" (TUF), played a significant role in expanding the UFC's reach. TUF series were launched in various countries, including the United States, Brazil, Australia, and more. These shows unearthed local talents, giving them a shot at UFC glory and fostering a global fan base.

A New Era: Asian Expansion

In 2010, the UFC made a significant move by venturing into the Asian market with UFC 144 in Saitama, Japan. This marked the beginning of an ongoing effort to tap into the Asian MMA scene. Events in countries like China, South Korea, and Singapore followed, solidifying the UFC's presence in the continent.

UFC Takes Over Europe

Europe became a hotbed for MMA talent, and the UFC capitalized on this by hosting events throughout the continent. Locations like Dublin, London, and Stockholm witnessed sold-out arenas as European fighters became prominent contenders in various weight classes.

Africa Joins the UFC Landscape

In recent years, the UFC has made inroads into Africa, showcasing the continent's MMA potential. Fighters like Israel Adesanya, Kamaru Usman, and Francis Ngannou have risen to prominence, drawing global attention to African talent.

Land of the Rising Octagon: UFC in Asia

The UFC's presence in Asia has grown significantly, with the organization hosting events in countries like China, South Korea, and Singapore. The rise of Asian fighters, including Zhang Weili and Kyoji Horiguchi, has contributed to the UFC's popularity in the region.

Continued Growth and Worldwide Impact

The UFC's expansion onto multiple continents has not only broadened its reach but also transformed MMA into a truly global sport. It has provided fighters from diverse backgrounds with a platform to showcase their skills and has created a passionate and dedicated international fan base.

A Global Fighting Spectacle

The UFC's journey from its American roots to its current status as a global sporting powerhouse is a testament to the appeal of mixed martial arts. With events spanning across continents, the organization has brought fans from all walks of life together to witness the world's best fighters compete inside the iconic Octagon. The UFC's worldwide reach has not only changed the face of MMA but has also enriched the lives of countless fighters and fans across the globe.

Chapter 48: The Art of Unique Fighting Styles

The sport of mixed martial arts (MMA) is a canvas for fighters to express their individuality. In this chapter, we'll delve into the fascinating world of UFC fighters' unique fighting stances and techniques, exploring how these distinct approaches have left an indelible mark on the sport.

The Evolution of MMA Styles

In the early days of the UFC, fighters often specialized in a single discipline, such as Brazilian Jiu-Jitsu or kickboxing. Over time, as the sport evolved, fighters began to cross-train in various disciplines, leading to the emergence of hybrid fighting styles.

"The Spider" Anderson Silva's Matrix-Like Moves

Anderson Silva, a former UFC Middleweight Champion, is known for his uncanny ability to dodge strikes with fluid head movement and agility reminiscent of a character from "The Matrix." His unique style allowed him to evade opponents' attacks and counter with precision.

Lyoto "The Dragon" Machida's Karate-Based Style

Lyoto Machida, a former UFC Light Heavyweight Champion, introduced a karate-based fighting style that emphasized elusive footwork and counterstriking. His unorthodox approach made him a difficult puzzle for opponents to solve.

Conor McGregor's Precision Striking

Conor McGregor, a former UFC Featherweight and Lightweight Champion, is celebrated for his striking accuracy. McGregor's left hand, known as the "Celtic Cross," has delivered devastating knockouts. His fighting stance is often wide and bladed, allowing him to generate significant power in his punches.

Dominick Cruz's Unpredictable Footwork

Dominick Cruz, a former UFC Bantamweight Champion, is renowned for his unpredictable footwork and stance-switching. He confounds opponents with rapid movement, making him a difficult target to hit. His style is a testament to the importance of footwork in MMA.

Tony Ferguson's Unconventional Tactics

Tony Ferguson, known as "El Cucuy," is one of the most unpredictable fighters in the UFC. His fighting style incorporates unorthodox strikes, grappling, and a relentless pace. Ferguson's creativity inside the Octagon has led to his success.

"The Karate Hottie" Michelle Waterson's Versatility

Michelle Waterson, nicknamed "The Karate Hottie," possesses a diverse skill set. Her karate background is evident in her striking, but she's equally proficient in submissions. Her ability to seamlessly transition between techniques makes her a unique fighter.

Israel Adesanya's Striking Brilliance

Israel Adesanya, the reigning UFC Middleweight Champion, is a striking prodigy. He combines elements of kickboxing and traditional martial arts in his style, utilizing precise kicks and punches to keep opponents at bay.

Jon Jones' Unmatched Adaptability

Jon Jones, the former UFC Light Heavyweight Champion, is known for his adaptability. His fighting style can change from fight to fight, making him a versatile and unpredictable opponent. Jones has used various techniques, from wrestling to striking, to dominate his rivals.

The Artistry of Uniqueness

UFC fighters' unique fighting stances and techniques are a testament to the sport's evolution. Each fighter brings their own style, personality, and creativity to the Octagon, captivating fans worldwide. Whether it's Anderson Silva's matrix-like moves or Dominick Cruz's unpredictable footwork, these distinctive approaches contribute to the beauty and diversity of MMA. As fighters continue to innovate and push boundaries,

MMA remains an ever-evolving and endlessly fascinating combat sport.

Chapter 49: A Sport in the Crosshairs

The emergence of mixed martial arts (MMA) in the early 1990s was marked by its raw, unbridled violence, captivating some and alarming others. In this chapter, we delve into the turbulent early years of the sport as it quickly drew the attention of U.S. authorities.

The Birth of the UFC and its Controversial Reception

The first Ultimate Fighting Championship (UFC) event in 1993 was a spectacle of martial arts, showcasing fighters of various disciplines pitted against each other in a quest for supremacy. However, the UFC's "no-holds-barred" format raised concerns about fighter safety and the promotion's moral implications.

Political and Public Outcry

As the UFC gained popularity, it faced growing opposition from politicians, media outlets, and advocacy groups. Critics argued that the sport was too violent and lacked adequate regulation. This outcry led to legal challenges and threats of government intervention.

John McCain's Crusade Against MMA

One of the most vocal opponents of MMA in its early days was Senator John McCain. He referred to the sport as "human cockfighting" and called for its ban.

McCain's efforts to curtail MMA led to a crackdown on the sport in several states.

UFC 12: The First Step Towards Regulation

Amid mounting pressure, the UFC took steps to address safety concerns. UFC 12, held in 1997, introduced weight classes and additional rules, signaling a shift toward greater regulation. These changes were crucial in the UFC's bid for legitimacy.

State Athletic Commissions and the Unified Rules

To gain acceptance and avoid government intervention, the UFC cooperated with state athletic commissions. In 2000, the New Jersey State Athletic Control Board implemented the Unified Rules of Mixed Martial Arts, a comprehensive set of regulations that became the industry standard.

Zuffa LLC: A Turning Point

The UFC's fortunes changed when Zuffa LLC, led by Lorenzo and Frank Fertitta and Dana White, purchased the organization in 2001. Zuffa's commitment to regulation, fighter safety, and professionalism helped the UFC overcome its troubled past.

A Sport's Evolution

The early years of MMA were marked by controversy and opposition. However, through a combination of self-regulation, cooperation with state athletic commissions, and the UFC's commitment to reform, the sport evolved into a respected and globally recognized athletic competition. While its roots are entangled with violence, MMA's journey toward legitimacy reflects its capacity to adapt, grow, and transform into a mainstream sport embraced by millions worldwide.

Chapter 50: The Rise of Interim Titles

In the world of combat sports, champions are revered for their exceptional skill and dedication. However, injuries, personal issues, or contractual disputes can sometimes force champions to step away from the Octagon. To maintain the integrity of their divisions, the UFC introduced interim titles, a concept that has generated its own share of debate and excitement.

Champion Absence and the Need for Interim Titles

The UFC's decision to introduce interim titles was largely driven by the need to keep divisions active and maintain fan interest when a reigning champion was unavailable. Whether due to injuries or other circumstances, champion absences posed a challenge to the promotion.

The Birth of Interim Titles

The first interim title bout took place at UFC 43 in 2003. It featured Randy Couture facing off against the formidable Pedro Rizzo for the interim heavyweight title. Couture's victory not only signaled the birth of interim titles but also demonstrated their significance in the UFC.

Interim Titles in the Modern Era

Over the years, interim titles became more common in the UFC, especially as the promotion expanded its global reach. Fighters like Tony Ferguson, Max Holloway, and Colby Covington have all held interim belts during their careers, adding layers of intrigue to their respective divisions.

Controversies Surrounding Interim Titles

While interim titles have been celebrated for keeping divisions active, they have also faced criticism. Some argue that their proliferation diminishes the value of a championship belt, while others believe they can create confusion about the true champion of a division.

Notable Interim Title Bouts

Several memorable interim title fights have taken place, with fighters often displaying remarkable skills and determination. These bouts have served as a testament to the fighters' abilities and their desire to prove themselves as the best in their weight classes.

Interim Titles and the Unified Championship

When a fighter holding an interim title gets the opportunity to challenge the reigning champion, it often results in a unification bout. These high-stakes matchups showcase the best fighters in the division, ultimately leading to a single undisputed champion.

Balancing Act

The introduction of interim titles in the UFC has been both celebrated and criticized. While they serve a vital role in maintaining divisional activity and providing opportunities to fighters, their overuse or misuse can lead to confusion and controversy. Nonetheless, they remain an integral part of the sport's evolving landscape, offering a glimpse into the delicate balance between tradition and innovation that defines the UFC and MMA as a whole.

Chapter 51: Dominick Cruz - The Footwork Maestro

In the world of mixed martial arts, fighters often become known for their distinctive styles and techniques. Dominick Cruz, with his exceptional footwork and fighting style, is one such fighter who has left an indelible mark on the sport. His approach to combat combines movement, strategy, and adaptability in a way that few can match.

Early Years and Wrestling Roots

Dominick Cruz's journey into the world of MMA began with a strong foundation in wrestling. He honed his grappling skills in his youth and later transitioned into mixed martial arts. His wrestling background provided him with a solid base upon which to build his unique fighting style.

The Signature Footwork

What sets Cruz apart from many fighters is his extraordinary footwork. He employs constant lateral movement, shifting angles, and unpredictable feints to confound opponents. This elusive style allows him to evade strikes while positioning himself to land counterattacks effectively.

Dominance in the WEC

Cruz's early career in the World Extreme Cagefighting (WEC) promotion showcased his developing skills. He climbed the ranks and secured the WEC Bantamweight Championship in 2010, solidifying himself as one of the best in the division.

UFC Success and the Bantamweight Throne

When the UFC absorbed the WEC, Cruz carried his championship and style into the larger promotion. He continued to showcase his footwork wizardry while defending his title. His rivalry with Urijah Faber and their trilogy of fights added another layer of excitement to his career.

Injury Woes and Comebacks

Cruz's UFC career was marred by a series of injuries that forced him to relinquish his title. These setbacks could have deterred many fighters, but Cruz's determination was unwavering. He embarked on long and grueling comebacks, showcasing his resilience.

The Epic Return and Reclaiming the Throne

Perhaps one of the most memorable moments in Cruz's career was his return to the Octagon after a three-year layoff due to injuries. He faced TJ Dillashaw, who had claimed the bantamweight title in his absence. Cruz's victory in a close and thrilling bout demonstrated his ability to adapt and overcome adversity.

Legacy and Influence

Dominick Cruz's fighting style has had a lasting impact on the sport. Many fighters, both aspiring and established, have studied and incorporated elements of his footwork into their own arsenals. His legacy extends beyond championships and victories; it encompasses the artistry of movement in combat.

The Footwork Legacy

Dominick Cruz's exceptional footwork and fighting style have made him a revered figure in MMA. His ability to blend precision, adaptability, and elusive movement has left an indomitable mark on the sport. As a fighter, a champion, and an innovator, Cruz's contributions to the world of mixed martial arts will continue to be celebrated and studied by generations of fighters and fans alike.

Chapter 52: Diverse Origins, One Octagon

The Ultimate Fighting Championship (UFC) stands as a testament to the global reach of mixed martial arts (MMA). With fighters hailing from diverse backgrounds, nationalities, and cultures, the Octagon is a vibrant mosaic where different stories, styles, and experiences converge to create the electrifying spectacle that is the UFC.

The International Phenomenon

From its humble beginnings in the United States, the UFC quickly expanded its horizons. The promotion's willingness to embrace talent from around the world contributed to its exponential growth. Today, the UFC hosts fighters from nearly every corner of the globe, making it a truly international phenomenon.

A Brazilian Jiu-Jitsu Revolution

The UFC's early years were marked by the dominance of Brazilian fighters. Legends like Royce Gracie, Anderson Silva, and Antonio Rodrigo Nogueira introduced the world to the art of Brazilian Jiu-Jitsu. Their success played a pivotal role in popularizing submission grappling and showcasing the global appeal of MMA.

Eastern Europe's Rise

Eastern Europe emerged as a formidable MMA hub with fighters like Fedor Emelianenko, Mirko Cro Cop, and Khabib Nurmagomedov achieving worldwide acclaim. These athletes brought a unique blend of combat sports, often rooted in wrestling and sambo, to the Octagon.

The Impact of Western Wrestling

Wrestling, particularly the American collegiate style, has produced a plethora of UFC talent. Fighters like Randy Couture, Dan Henderson, and Daniel Cormier showcased the effectiveness of wrestling in MMA, opening the door for numerous other wrestlers to transition into the sport.

Asian Influence and Martial Arts Traditions

Asia has a rich history of martial arts, and fighters from the continent have left their mark on the UFC. Names like Kazushi Sakuraba, Wanderlei Silva, and more recently, Zhang Weili, have showcased the striking and grappling arts of the East.

The Canadian Connection

Canada has consistently produced top-tier fighters, with Georges St-Pierre and Rory MacDonald being prime examples. These athletes have demonstrated a well-rounded approach to MMA, combining striking, grappling, and strong conditioning.

African Pioneers

Africa has recently emerged as a hotbed of talent, with fighters like Israel Adesanya and Kamaru Usman capturing titles. Their athleticism, striking skills, and relentless work ethic have put the continent on the MMA map.

The Oceania Wave

Australia and New Zealand have seen a surge in MMA interest, with fighters like Robert Whittaker and Israel Adesanya becoming world champions. The Oceanic fighters often bring a blend of striking arts such as boxing and kickboxing to the Octagon.

A Global Tapestry of Fighters

The UFC's appeal lies in its ability to transcend borders and cultures. It's a place where fighters from diverse backgrounds come together, each contributing a unique thread to the global tapestry of MMA. This rich mosaic of talent ensures that the UFC remains a dynamic, ever-evolving sport that reflects the universal language of combat. As the promotion continues to grow, one thing is certain: the Octagon will always be a place where the world comes to fight.

Chapter 53: Unearthing "The Diamond"

In the world of mixed martial arts (MMA), fighters often adopt monikers or nicknames that encapsulate their journey, character, or fighting style. One such fighter, Dustin Poirier, is known as "The Diamond." This moniker not only hints at his resilience and growth but also serves as a testament to his enduring presence in the Ultimate Fighting Championship (UFC).

A Fighter's Beginnings

Dustin Poirier was born on January 19, 1989, in Lafayette, Louisiana, USA. His journey into the world of combat sports began at a young age when he started training in boxing. This initial foray into pugilism laid the foundation for what would become a remarkable MMA career.

The Crucible of the Fight Game

Poirier began his professional MMA career in 2009, competing in various promotions before earning a spot in the prestigious WEC (World Extreme Cagefighting). There, he showcased his striking prowess and tenacity, earning respect from fans and fellow fighters alike.

A UFC Arrival and Early Challenges

In 2011, Poirier transitioned to the UFC, where he faced a steep learning curve. His early fights in the promotion were marked by a mix of victories and setbacks, highlighting the unforgiving nature of the sport. However, these experiences served as stepping stones for his growth.

The Diamond Emerges

As Poirier continued to evolve as a fighter, the nickname "The Diamond" began to take on new significance. Diamonds are formed under immense pressure, and Poirier's ability to shine brightly under the pressure of high-stakes fights became evident.

Iconic Battles and Redemption

Throughout his career, Dustin Poirier has engaged in memorable clashes with some of the sport's biggest names, including Justin Gaethje, Max Holloway, and Eddie Alvarez. These battles not only showcased his technical prowess but also his heart and determination.

The Trilogy with Conor McGregor

Poirier's name became etched in MMA history during his rivalry with Conor McGregor. Their trilogy of fights showcased Poirier's adaptability and his ability to make strategic adjustments. His victory over McGregor in UFC 257 was a career-defining moment, earning him widespread recognition.

The Giving Fighter

Beyond his fighting skills, Poirier is known for his philanthropy. He established "The Good Fight

Foundation," which focuses on helping communities and individuals in need. His commitment to making a positive impact outside the cage exemplifies the qualities of a true champion.

A Shining Gem

Dustin Poirier's journey from a young boy in Lafayette, Louisiana, to a UFC superstar known as "The Diamond" is a testament to his dedication, perseverance, and ability to thrive under pressure. His legacy in the sport will forever be marked not only by his exciting fights but also by his contributions to the well-being of others. As "The Diamond" continues to shine, his story remains an inspiration to fighters and fans alike, reminding us that resilience and growth are qualities that can turn ordinary individuals into gems in the world of MMA.

Chapter 54: UFC's High-Altitude Adventures

In the world of the Ultimate Fighting Championship (UFC), fighters often face unique challenges that test their mettle. One such challenge arises when UFC events are held in high-altitude locations. These venues, typically situated above sea level, add an extra layer of complexity to the already grueling sport of mixed martial arts (MMA).

The Impact of High Altitude

High-altitude locations, defined as areas situated 5,000 feet (approximately 1,524 meters) or higher above sea level, present several physiological challenges to fighters. The lower oxygen levels at these altitudes can affect cardiovascular performance, stamina, and overall physical endurance. When fighters step into the Octagon at such venues, they must confront not only their opponents but also the thin mountain air.

UFC's High-Altitude Adventures

The UFC has ventured into high-altitude locations on multiple occasions, offering fans and fighters the thrill of experiencing MMA in these unique settings. While not an exhaustive list, here are a few notable instances where the UFC showcased its brand of combat sports at high altitudes:

UFC Fight Night: Maia vs. Condit (August 2016) - Mexico City, Mexico (7,382 feet/2,250 meters)

One of the most well-known high-altitude events in UFC history took place in Mexico City. At an elevation of over 7,000 feet, this event challenged fighters' ability to adapt to the reduced oxygen levels. Carlos Condit and Demian Maia headlined the card, putting on a thrilling fight that went the distance, testing their cardio and endurance in the thin air.

UFC Fight Night: Ortega vs. The Korean Zombie (October 2019) - Busan, South Korea (13 feet/4 meters)

While not a high-altitude location, this event marked the other end of the spectrum, as it was held in Busan, South Korea, at sea level. Fighters who had previously competed at high altitudes faced an entirely different challenge: the increased oxygen levels could lead to faster-paced fights, demanding constant action and a high level of aggression.

UFC Fight Night: Poirier vs. Hooker (June 2020) - Las Vegas, Nevada (2,001 feet/610 meters)

Although Las Vegas is not typically considered a high-altitude location, the UFC's APEX facility is located at an elevation of around 2,000 feet above sea level. Fighters competing here have noted differences in cardio and endurance compared to sea-level venues, adding an intriguing variable to their performances.

Adaptation and Strategy

Competing at high altitudes requires fighters and their teams to adapt their training and fight strategies. Many athletes choose to arrive at these locations well in advance to acclimatize to the reduced oxygen levels. Training sessions often include specialized techniques to improve lung capacity and cardiovascular endurance.

The Altitude Challenge

UFC events in high-altitude locations add a unique layer of complexity to the already intense world of MMA. Fighters who step into the Octagon at these venues must not only contend with their opponents but also adapt to the thin mountain air. These high-altitude adventures offer fans unforgettable moments and showcase the adaptability and resilience of fighters, proving once again that in the UFC, the challenges never cease to amaze.

Chapter 55: UFC 5 - The Superfight Showdown

The early days of the Ultimate Fighting Championship (UFC) were characterized by innovation, unpredictability, and the clash of martial arts styles. UFC 5, which took place on April 7, 1995, at the Independence Arena in Charlotte, North Carolina, was no exception. This event is particularly remembered for introducing the first singles match, "The Superfight," a rematch between two legends of the sport, Royce Gracie and Ken Shamrock.

The Fighters: Royce Gracie vs. Ken Shamrock

Royce Gracie, a Brazilian Jiu-Jitsu master and a member of the Gracie family, had become an iconic figure in the early days of the UFC. He had won the first two UFC tournaments (UFC 1 and UFC 2) with his exceptional grappling skills. On the other side of the Octagon stood Ken Shamrock, a skilled submission specialist with a strong wrestling background. Their first encounter at UFC 1 had ended in a draw due to time limits, and fans were eager to see them face off again.

The Superfight Build-Up

The anticipation leading up to the Superfight was palpable. Both Gracie and Shamrock had grown as fighters since their first meeting, and fans were curious to see how the rematch would unfold. Gracie had already secured three UFC tournament victories, while Shamrock was a formidable opponent with a reputation for his submission skills and toughness.

The Fight: Disappointment in the Octagon

While the rematch had the potential to be an epic showdown, it ultimately left many fans disappointed. The Superfight at UFC 5 ended in a 36-minute time-limit draw. This result, combined with the lack of action in the match, did not meet the expectations of fans who had hoped for a definitive conclusion to their rivalry.

The disappointment stemmed from several factors, including the absence of a clear winner, the extended duration of the fight, and the limited action. The fight primarily took place on the ground, with both fighters attempting submissions but unable to secure a victory.

Legacy and Impact

The Superfight between Royce Gracie and Ken Shamrock remains a significant moment in UFC history. It highlighted the need for time limits and rules to prevent excessively long matches with no resolution. This bout also laid the foundation for the eventual introduction of judges' decisions in UFC fights.

Despite the disappointment of the rematch itself, the Gracie-Shamrock rivalry played a pivotal role in building the UFC's early fan base. It showcased the clash of different martial arts disciplines and set the stage for the evolution of mixed martial arts as a sport.

A Pioneering Match

UFC 5's Superfight between Royce Gracie and Ken Shamrock, while considered a disappointment due to its inconclusive ending and prolonged duration, was a pioneering moment in the history of the UFC. It reflected the sport's early experimental phase and the evolving rules and regulations that would ultimately shape modern MMA. This bout between two legends of the sport remains a pivotal chapter in the annals of the UFC's journey from its inception to its current status as a global phenomenon.

Chapter 56: UFC Fight Pass - A Gateway to MMA

In the digital age of sports entertainment, fans demand immediate access to their favorite content. Recognizing this shift in consumer behavior, the Ultimate Fighting Championship (UFC) launched UFC Fight Pass, a subscription-based streaming service, in December 2013. This marked a significant step forward in the organization's efforts to connect with fans worldwide and provide them with a comprehensive library of mixed martial arts (MMA) content.

Unlimited Access to the World of MMA

UFC Fight Pass was designed to offer MMA enthusiasts unprecedented access to a vast array of content. Subscribers gain access to an extensive library of past UFC events, including early classics and recent main cards. Beyond the UFC, the service features a wide range of content from various MMA promotions, showcasing the best fights and fighters from around the globe.

Original and Exclusive Programming

UFC Fight Pass doesn't just serve as a repository for archived fights; it also produces its own original content. Subscribers can enjoy exclusive series, documentaries, and behind-the-scenes footage, providing an intimate look into the lives and training camps of their favorite fighters.

One of the most popular features of UFC Fight Pass is "Dana White's Contender Series," where up-and-coming fighters compete for a chance to earn a UFC contract. This series has not only introduced fresh talent to the UFC but has also become a fan-favorite due to its focus on prospects with something to prove.

Live Events and Early Prelims

In addition to its library of past fights and original programming, UFC Fight Pass offers live streaming of certain events. This includes early prelims for select UFC events, which are typically not available on cable or pay-per-view broadcasts. This has been a game-changer for fans who want to catch all the action from the very beginning of an event.

International Appeal

UFC Fight Pass has expanded its reach globally, making it accessible to fans around the world. The service is available in numerous countries, and its content is localized to cater to different regions, languages, and cultures. This international approach has helped the UFC grow its global fan base and reach new audiences.

A Growing Legacy

Since its inception, UFC Fight Pass has continued to evolve. It has adapted to fan feedback, expanded its content library, and improved its user interface to provide a seamless viewing experience. The service has become an essential tool for both hardcore MMA fans and newcomers looking to explore the world of combat sports.

A Cornerstone of UFC Fandom

UFC Fight Pass has emerged as a cornerstone of UFC fandom, offering fans an all-encompassing portal into the world of MMA. It has not only preserved the history of the sport but has also propelled it into the digital age, providing fans with an ever-expanding universe of content. As the UFC continues to grow and evolve, so too will UFC Fight Pass, ensuring that fans can stay connected to the sport they love, anytime and anywhere.

Chapter 57: From Octagon to Silver Screen - UFC Fighters Turned Actors

UFC fighters are known for their incredible athleticism, courage, and fighting skills, but many have also ventured into the world of acting and entertainment. This chapter explores the fascinating journey of UFC fighters who made the transition from the Octagon to the silver screen, bringing their charisma, discipline, and star power to a new stage.

Randy Couture: The Natural Actor

Randy "The Natural" Couture is a prime example of a UFC fighter who successfully crossed over into acting. After a storied career in the Octagon, where he became a multi-division champion, Couture transitioned to Hollywood. He made his acting debut in "The Scorpion King 2: Rise of a Warrior" and went on to star in action films like "The Expendables" series alongside Sylvester Stallone. Couture's rugged charm and physicality made him a sought-after talent in the entertainment industry.

Quinton "Rampage" Jackson: A Prolific Film Career

Quinton "Rampage" Jackson, known for his explosive fighting style, made a name for himself not only in the UFC but also in Hollywood. He gained prominence with his role as B.A. Baracus in the 2010 film adaptation of "The A-Team." Jackson's larger-than-life personality and imposing presence translated seamlessly to the big screen, earning him roles in various action films and television series.

Gina Carano: From MMA to Star Wars

Gina Carano, a former MMA fighter and one of the pioneering women in the sport, made a significant leap to acting. She gained acclaim for her role in Steven Soderbergh's "Haywire" and appeared in action-packed films like "Fast & Furious 6." Carano's acting career reached new heights when she joined the Star Wars universe as Cara Dune in the Disney+ series "The Mandalorian." Her transition showcased her versatility and ability to excel in both combat sports and entertainment.

Chuck Liddell: Lights Out on Screen

Chuck "The Iceman" Liddell, a UFC Hall of Famer and former light heavyweight champion, ventured into acting after his fighting career. His notable appearances include roles in films such as "Kick-Ass 2" and TV series like "Hawaii Five-o." Liddell's popularity from his UFC days and his intimidating presence made him a natural fit for action-packed roles.

Ronda Rousey: Breaking Boundaries in Hollywood

Ronda Rousey, the trailblazing UFC Women's Bantamweight Champion, became a household name not only for her fighting prowess but also for her acting career. She made her acting debut in "The Expendables 3" and went on to appear in films like "Furious 7" and "Mile 22." Rousey's charisma and fearless attitude transcended the Octagon, earning her a prominent place in the entertainment industry.

Fighters Turned Entertainers

The journey from being a UFC fighter to an actor or entertainer is a testament to the multifaceted talents of these individuals. These fighters, known for their physical toughness, have showcased their adaptability and charisma in the world of entertainment. Their successful transitions not only expand their horizons but also bring a unique blend of intensity and authenticity to the silver screen, captivating audiences worldwide.

Chapter 58: Inside the Octagon - Embedded Journalism in the UFC

The Ultimate Fighting Championship (UFC) is not only a powerhouse in the world of mixed martial arts but also a pioneer in sports media coverage. One of its most innovative approaches to media is the "Embedded" series, which provides fans with unprecedented access to fighters, their teams, and the behind-the-scenes action leading up to a fight. This chapter delves into the world of embedded journalism in the UFC and its impact on both fans and fighters.

The Birth of Embedded: A Glimpse Behind the Curtain

The "Embedded" series was introduced as part of the UFC's efforts to offer fans a more immersive experience. It was designed to take viewers on a journey from the fighters' training camps to the fight night itself. The series allows fans to see the emotional and physical preparation that goes into each bout.

Unprecedented Access: Life in Training Camps

One of the most compelling aspects of the "Embedded" series is its access to fighters' training camps. Embedded journalists capture the grueling workouts, sparring sessions, and strategic discussions that shape a fighter's preparation. This level of transparency has allowed fans to gain a deeper understanding of the dedication and sacrifice required to compete at the highest level of MMA.

Fighter Profiles: Personal Stories Unfold

Embedded journalists don't just focus on training; they also delve into the personal lives of fighters. These segments reveal the human side of combat sports, showcasing the fighters' families, hobbies, and motivations. This personalized approach has endeared fighters to fans on a more profound level, creating a stronger emotional connection.

Fight Week: The Final Countdown

As fight night approaches, "Embedded" provides exclusive access to the fighters' experiences during fight week. From the weight cut to the weigh-ins and media obligations, fans get a front-row seat to the rollercoaster of emotions that fighters go through in the days leading up to their bouts. This inside look amplifies the anticipation for the actual fight.

Fan Engagement: Fostering a Dedicated Community

The "Embedded" series has become a vital tool for fan engagement. It generates excitement, discussion, and anticipation on social media platforms and the UFC's official website. Fans eagerly await each new episode, turning the lead-up to a fight into a shared experience.

Fighter Autonomy: Crafting Their Narratives

Embedded journalism also allows fighters to take control of their narratives. They can use the series to showcase their personalities, promote their personal brands, and connect with fans on their own terms. This autonomy has empowered fighters in the digital age.

A Game-Changer in Sports Media

The UFC's "Embedded" series has revolutionized sports media by offering an unprecedented level of access and storytelling. It has transformed the way fans engage with the sport and the fighters, creating a sense of intimacy and connection. As the UFC continues to evolve, its commitment to media innovation ensures that fans will remain at the forefront of the action, both inside and outside the Octagon.

Chapter 59: The Art of Pre-Fight Trash Talk in the UFC

In the world of mixed martial arts, pre-fight trash talk is a well-established tradition. Fighters, fueled by adrenaline and the desire to assert dominance, engage in verbal warfare to hype up their bouts. This chapter explores the art of pre-fight trash talk in the UFC, featuring iconic figures like Conor McGregor and Chael Sonnen.

Setting the Stage: The Importance of Hype

The UFC, like any other sports organization, understands the value of promotion. Exciting fights draw viewers and generate revenue. Pre-fight trash talk serves as a tool to build anticipation, creating a narrative around a match that fans can invest in emotionally.

Chael Sonnen: The American Gangster

Chael Sonnen is often regarded as one of the pioneers of modern MMA trash talk. His gift of gab and quick wit made him a standout figure in the sport. Sonnen's infamous feud with Anderson Silva, which spanned two championship bouts, showcased his ability to sell fights through words alone. His brash demeanor and over-the-top confidence made him a polarizing but undeniably compelling figure.

Conor McGregor: The Notorious Showman

Conor McGregor took the art of trash talk to new heights. His magnetic personality and gift for the gab helped him transcend the sport of MMA. McGregor's legendary verbal duels with opponents like Jose Aldo, Nate Diaz, and Khabib Nurmagomedov not only boosted pay-per-view numbers but also solidified his status as a global superstar. His brash predictions and relentless self-promotion became iconic elements of his persona.

The Psychological Game: Getting Inside Your Opponent's Head

Pre-fight trash talk is more than just entertainment; it's a psychological weapon. Fighters aim to destabilize their opponents mentally, creating doubt and anxiety. When done effectively, it can give them a mental edge before they even step into the Octagon. By crafting a narrative of superiority, fighters attempt to convince not only their opponents but also themselves that victory is inevitable.

The Line Between Hype and Disrespect

While trash talk is a fundamental part of the fight game, it can sometimes cross into disrespectful territory. Personal attacks and offensive comments have caused controversies in the past. Fighters must strike a delicate balance between hyping a fight and maintaining mutual respect.

The Post-Fight Reckoning: Backing Up the Talk

Ultimately, pre-fight trash talk sets high expectations for the fighters. When the cage door closes, they must deliver on their promises. Failure to do so can damage their credibility and popularity. Conversely, a fighter who backs up their talk with a dominant performance becomes a more significant force in the sport.

The Artistry of Fight Hype

Pre-fight trash talk is a double-edged sword in the world of MMA. When wielded skillfully, it can elevate fighters' profiles, generate buzz, and enhance the fan experience. However, it must be approached with caution, as the line between hype and disrespect is razor-thin. In the end, it's an integral part of the theater that surrounds every great fight, adding layers of drama and anticipation to the spectacle that is the UFC.

Chapter 60: The UFC-WWE Crossover: Stars Who Shined in Both Worlds

The worlds of professional wrestling and mixed martial arts might seem vastly different, but there exists a unique crossover between them. Some fighters have successfully transitioned between the UFC and WWE, demonstrating their versatility and ability to capture the attention of fans in two distinct forms of combat entertainment. This chapter delves into the stories of two prominent figures in this crossover: Brock Lesnar and Ronda Rousey.

Brock Lesnar: The Beast Incarnate

Brock Lesnar's journey from the UFC Octagon to the WWE ring and back is nothing short of remarkable. Known as "The Beast Incarnate," Lesnar is a physical specimen with a background in collegiate wrestling. He made his UFC debut in 2008 and quickly rose through the ranks, winning the UFC Heavyweight Championship. His brute strength, explosive athleticism, and raw power made him a formidable force.

After his initial stint in the UFC, Lesnar returned to the WWE, where he had previously enjoyed a successful career. He became one of the promotion's biggest draws, headlining major events and holding the WWE Universal Championship multiple times. Lesnar's ability to seamlessly switch between the scripted world of wrestling and the unforgiving realm of MMA is a testament to his exceptional talent and charisma.

Ronda Rousey: The Rowdy One

Ronda Rousey, often referred to as "The Baddest Woman on the Planet," made her mark in the UFC as the first Women's Bantamweight Champion. Her dominance and quick victories in the Octagon captured the imagination of fans worldwide. Rousey's judo background, combined with her relentless aggression, made her a transcendent figure in MMA.

In 2018, Rousey transitioned to the WWE, where she became a central figure in the women's division. Her crossover was marked by high-profile matches and a memorable run as the WWE Raw Women's Champion. Rousey's charisma, natural athleticism, and ability to connect with audiences carried over from the Octagon to the squared circle.

The Appeal of the Crossover

The success of fighters like Brock Lesnar and Ronda Rousey in both the UFC and WWE highlights the entertainment value and star power that they bring to both worlds. Their ability to captivate audiences, whether in real combat or scripted storytelling, demonstrates the enduring appeal of combat sports.

The Challenges of Transition

Transitioning between the UFC and WWE is not without its challenges. While the physicality and combat skills are transferable, the scripted nature of professional wrestling demands a different set of performance skills. Learning the art of storytelling through scripted promos and matches can be a steep learning curve for fighters accustomed to the authenticity of MMA.

Legends in Two Arenas

Brock Lesnar and Ronda Rousey's journeys between the UFC and WWE underscore the versatility and star power of elite fighters. Their ability to thrive in two distinct forms of combat sports is a testament to their talent and charisma. While not all fighters can make such a transition, these two stand as iconic examples of success in both the Octagon and the wrestling ring, bridging the gap between the real and the scripted in combat entertainment.

Chapter 61: Fighting Al Fresco: UFC's Outdoor Arena Extravaganzas

While the UFC typically finds its home inside arenas and stadiums, the promotion has, on several occasions, ventured into the open air, hosting events in outdoor arenas. These unique shows offer a distinct atmosphere, blending the excitement of mixed martial arts with the elements of nature. This chapter explores the experiences and challenges associated with UFC events in outdoor venues.

Unconventional Settings

The UFC has never been one to shy away from trying new things, and hosting events outdoors is no exception. These events have taken place in various locations, from beachfronts to city parks, creating a fresh and sometimes unexpected backdrop for MMA action.

Challenges of the Elements

Outdoor events present challenges that are absent in the controlled environment of indoor arenas. Weather can be a significant factor, with the potential for rain, wind, extreme heat, or cold. Fighters and organizers must adapt to these conditions, which can affect everything from fighter performance to the safety of the audience.

Memorable Outdoor UFC Events

1. **UFC 146 - May 26, 2012:** This event took place at the MGM Grand Garden Arena in Las Vegas, but the main card featured all heavyweight bouts. It's fondly remembered for its lineup of big men slugging it out.
2. **UFC Fight Island - July 11, 2020:** While not fully outdoors, this series of events held on Yas Island in Abu Dhabi included outdoor elements, such as the famous "Fight Island" octagon on the beach. It was a unique endeavor necessitated by the COVID-19 pandemic.
3. **UFC on Fox 14 - January 24, 2015:** This event in Stockholm, Sweden, was held in the Tele2 Arena, an indoor stadium with a retractable roof. However, the roof was open, and the event had an outdoor feel, with chilly Scandinavian temperatures.

The Audience Experience

Outdoor events often provide a different experience for fans. The connection to nature and the open space can create an exhilarating atmosphere. However, it's essential to ensure spectator comfort, especially in extreme weather conditions.

Safety Concerns

The safety of fighters and spectators is paramount in any UFC event, but the challenges posed by outdoor venues require additional precautions. Measures like appropriate lighting, temperature control, and contingency plans for weather-related issues must be in place.

A Breath of Fresh Air for MMA

UFC events in outdoor arenas bring a touch of adventure to the world of mixed martial arts. While they come with unique challenges, they also offer a chance to experience the sport in a different, sometimes more visceral way. These outdoor extravaganzas serve as a reminder that, in the UFC, even the sky is not the limit when it comes to showcasing the world's most exciting combat sport.

Chapter 62: Decisions, Disagreements, and Controversies: Judging in the UFC

In the world of mixed martial arts, a fight's outcome often rests in the hands of judges. The UFC has witnessed its fair share of incredible battles, but it has also been the stage for numerous controversial judging decisions. This chapter delves into the complexities of scoring fights, the nature of controversies, and the steps taken by the UFC to address these issues.

The 10-Point Must System

The UFC primarily uses the 10-Point Must System for scoring fights. Under this system, judges award the winner of each round 10 points, with the opponent receiving 9 points or fewer, depending on their performance. The fighter with the most rounds won emerges as the victor, with a draw occurring if the scorecards are even.

Controversial Decisions: The Nature of the Beast

Controversial judging decisions can arise from a range of factors, including differences in judging criteria interpretation, hometown bias, or simple human error. Some of the most notorious UFC fights marred by controversial decisions include:

1. **Robbie Lawler vs. Carlos Condit (UFC 195):** A closely contested bout that saw Lawler

retain his welterweight title via split decision, but opinions on the outcome were divided among fans and analysts.
2. **Diego Sanchez vs. Ross Pearson (UFC Fight Night 42):** A bout in which Sanchez won via split decision, but many believed Pearson had done enough to secure the victory.
3. **Benson Henderson vs. Frankie Edgar (UFC 150):** In their rematch, Henderson won by a split decision that many fans and pundits found puzzling.

Addressing Controversies

The UFC and state athletic commissions have recognized the need to address judging controversies. Measures have been taken to improve the clarity of judging criteria, provide better training for judges, and increase transparency in scoring.

Open Scoring Experiment

In an effort to reduce controversies, the UFC experimented with open scoring in a few regional events. This system allowed fighters and coaches to know the judges' scores after each round, potentially affecting fight strategies and excitement.

The Introduction of Fight Stat Companions

To provide more context to fans and judges, the UFC introduced Fight Stat Companions, which display real-time statistics during a fight. While not an official scoring system, these stats can offer a clearer picture of a fight's progression.

Challenges Remain

Despite these efforts, judging controversies continue to be part of the sport. MMA's complexity and subjectivity make scoring a challenging task. The UFC, along with commissions, fighters, and fans, will continue to work towards refining the judging process and minimizing controversies.

Conclusion: The Ongoing Quest for Fairness

Controversial judging decisions are an intrinsic part of combat sports, including the UFC. While they can be frustrating, they also fuel discussions and debates among fans. The quest for fair and accurate judging remains an ongoing journey, reflecting the evolving nature of mixed martial arts as a sport.

Chapter 63: The Grand Stage: Fighter Entrances in the UFC

In the world of mixed martial arts, fighter entrances are a spectacle in their own right. These moments, filled with drama, anticipation, and raw emotion, serve as the prelude to the intense battles that will soon unfold inside the Octagon. This chapter delves into the captivating world of fighter entrances in the UFC.

The Walkout: A Fighter's Canvas

A fighter's entrance begins with the walkout, a unique opportunity to make a statement. The walkout is a canvas for self-expression, where fighters can showcase their personalities, cultures, and affiliations. Many fighters choose walkout music that resonates with them or their fanbase, adding a layer of emotional depth to their entrance.

Entrance Themes: The Soundtrack of Battle

Fighter entrance themes have become an iconic part of the UFC's storytelling. These songs are carefully chosen to evoke specific emotions and set the tone for the fight. Whether it's the pulsating beats of electronic music, the thunderous riffs of rock, or the rhythmic chants of traditional music, entrance themes are integral to a fighter's identity.

Lighting and Visual Effects

To heighten the drama, UFC events often feature dynamic lighting and visual effects during fighter entrances. Strobe lights, smoke, and lasers transform the arena into a breathtaking spectacle. These effects not only energize the crowd but also create a visually stunning backdrop for the fighters as they make their way to the Octagon.

Emotional Moments

Fighter entrances have produced some of the most emotional moments in UFC history. From the sheer intensity of Conor McGregor's strut to the heartfelt tributes to fallen loved ones, these entrances offer glimpses into the psyche of the fighters. They reveal the courage, determination, and vulnerability that define these warriors.

Iconic Entrances

Certain fighters have become known for their iconic entrances. The Undertaker-like presence of Anderson Silva, the Irish pride of Conor McGregor, or the "Last Emperor" Fedor Emelianenko's stoic walk—all of these have etched indelible memories in the minds of fans.

Cultural Significance

Fighter entrances often carry cultural significance. Fighters from around the world use their walkouts to pay homage to their heritage. Traditional clothing, flags, and music celebrate diversity and showcase the global nature of the sport.

Interactive Fan Experience

For fans attending live events, fighter entrances offer an interactive experience like no other. The crowd becomes part of the spectacle, chanting along with the music, waving flags, and creating an electrifying atmosphere that intensifies the moment.

The Artistry of the Entrance

In the world of the UFC, fighter entrances are not merely transitions from the locker room to the Octagon; they are a form of artistry, a blend of personal expression, cultural celebration, and emotional release. These moments, etched in the annals of MMA history, are an integral part of what makes the sport so captivating and unique.

Chapter 64: The Signature Walkout Attire of UFC Fighters

In the high-stakes world of the UFC, fighters understand the importance of making a statement not only inside the Octagon but also before they step foot in the cage. One of the most significant ways they did this prior to the Reebok deal, then later the Venum deal was through their signature walkout attire.

The Walkout Attire: Beyond Fashion

While walkout attire is, on the surface, a matter of fashion, it serves a much deeper purpose. It's not just about looking good; it's about feeling good, projecting confidence, and creating a lasting impression. Walkout attire often reflects a fighter's personality, culture, and mindset, and it can play a pivotal role in psyching out opponents.

Customization and Individuality

Every fighter's walkout attire was unique. From personalized colors and designs to sponsors' logos and team affiliations, these outfits showcase a fighter's individuality and serve as a canvas for self-expression. Some fighters even collaborate with designers to create one-of-a-kind pieces that resonate with their brand.

Sponsors and Branding

Sponsors played a significant role in a fighter's career, and walkout attire was one of the prime spaces for sponsor branding. Fighters could earn substantial income from sponsorships, and these partnerships often dictate the design and style of their walkout gear.

Symbolism and Cultural References

Fighters often used their walkout attire to convey messages or pay homage to their heritage. Flags, symbols, and phrases can hold deep cultural significance. For example, a fighter might have worn traditional clothing or adorn their attire with symbols that represent their roots or convey a particular message.

The Psychology of Attire

Walkout attire isn't just about aesthetics; it's about psychology. Fighters know that the mental game is as crucial as the physical one. They chose attire that empowers them, instills confidence, and sends a message to their opponent. A fighter who feels like a warrior before even entering the cage has a psychological advantage.

The Evolution of Walkout Attire

Over the years, walkout attire has evolved significantly. In the early days of the UFC, fighters often wore generic shorts and shirts. LaterToday, the attire is a high-stakes fashion statement, with elaborate designs, advanced materials, and a focus on functionality.

Now fighters are very limited to what they can wear through the present partnership with Venum.

Fan Engagement and Recognition

Fans eagerly anticipate a fighter's walkout, not just for the fight itself but in the past, also to catch a glimpse of their favorite athlete's signature attire. Iconic walkout outfits became etched in the collective memory of fans and add to a fighter's legacy.

Legal and Regulatory Aspects

The UFC has specific rules and regulations governing walkout attire. These rules ensure that attire is both functional and safe for fighters while also preventing any inappropriate or offensive content.

The Power of the Walkout Attire

In the world of the UFC, every detail matters, and walkout attire is no exception. It's a reflection of a fighter's identity, a canvas for self-expression, and a tool for psychological warfare. These custom outfits play a vital role in shaping a fighter's image, building their brand, and leaving an indelible mark on the minds of fans and opponents alike.

Chapter 65: The Exemplary Sportsmanship of Georges St-Pierre

Georges St-Pierre, affectionately known as "GSP," stands out not just for his incredible fighting skills but also for his exceptional sportsmanship and demeanor. This chapter delves into the remarkable career of Georges St-Pierre, highlighting his conduct inside and outside the Octagon that has earned him the respect and admiration of fans, fighters, and the entire MMA community.

The Early Days: A Humble Beginning

Georges St-Pierre was born on May 19, 1981, in Saint-Isidore, Quebec, Canada. He began training in Kyokushin karate at the age of seven, and from those early days, his dedication and respect for martial arts were evident. GSP's journey to becoming one of the greatest fighters in UFC history started with a strong foundation of discipline and sportsmanship.

Dominance in the Octagon

GSP's career in the UFC is nothing short of legendary. He captured the UFC Welterweight Championship twice and defended it nine times. His fighting style was a perfect blend of athleticism, technique, and intelligence. But what truly set him apart was his respect for his opponents.

The Gentleman Fighter

Inside the Octagon, Georges St-Pierre displayed an exceptional level of sportsmanship. He fought hard but always showed respect for his adversaries, win or lose. GSP's conduct during fights was a masterclass in honor and respect, setting an example for the entire MMA community.

The Aftermath of Victory and Defeat

GSP's demeanor after a fight was a testament to his character. When victorious, he would often console his defeated opponent, showing empathy and understanding for the physical and emotional challenges they had just faced. In defeat, he displayed grace and humility, acknowledging his opponent's skills and accepting responsibility for his performance.

Outside the Octagon: A Role Model

Beyond his fighting career, Georges St-Pierre continued to exhibit remarkable sportsmanship. He used his platform to promote the values of discipline, hard work, and respect for others. He became an ambassador for MMA, introducing the sport to a broader audience and dispelling misconceptions about its athletes.

The Impact on the Sport

GSP's sportsmanship and demeanor had a profound impact on the sport of MMA. He helped elevate its image, demonstrating that fighters could be both fierce competitors and exemplary sportsmen. His influence inspired a new generation of fighters to conduct themselves with honor and respect.

Legacy and Retirement

In 2013, Georges St-Pierre took a hiatus from MMA but returned in 2017 for a triumphant comeback, capturing the UFC Middleweight Championship. His legacy in the sport is secure, not only for his championships but also for his character. In February 2019, he announced his retirement from professional fighting, leaving behind a legacy of sportsmanship that will endure.

The Gentleman Who Redefined MMA

Georges St-Pierre's legacy extends far beyond his victories and championships. He redefined what it means to be a fighter in the brutal world of MMA, proving that sportsmanship, honor, and respect are as essential as any physical attribute. GSP's conduct inside and outside the Octagon has left an indelible mark on the sport, making him a role model for fighters and fans alike.

Chapter 66: The UFC's Digital Realm - YouTube Channel and Beyond

In the digital age, the Ultimate Fighting Championship (UFC) has embraced the power of the internet and social media to engage with fans and expand its reach. One of the cornerstones of this online presence is the UFC's YouTube channel. This chapter explores how the UFC leverages YouTube to share fight highlights, interviews, and behind-the-scenes content, providing fans with an immersive experience.

A Digital Hub for MMA Enthusiasts

The UFC's YouTube channel serves as a central hub for mixed martial arts (MMA) enthusiasts worldwide. With millions of subscribers and billions of views, it's evident that fans flock to the platform to get their dose of adrenaline-pumping action.

Fight Highlights: Reliving the Action

One of the primary draws of the UFC's YouTube channel is its extensive collection of fight highlights. After each event, the channel swiftly uploads bite-sized clips showcasing the most significant moments from every bout. Whether it's a brutal knockout, a slick submission, or a thrilling back-and-forth battle, these highlights allow fans to relive the excitement and drama of the fights.

Behind-the-Scenes Access: A Glimpse into Fighters' Lives

Beyond the Octagon, the UFC's YouTube channel offers fans a rare glimpse into the lives of their favorite fighters. Through interviews, vlogs, and documentaries, viewers can follow fighters on their journey from training camp to fight night. This behind-the-scenes content humanizes the athletes and builds a deeper connection between fighters and fans.

Embedded Series: The Ultimate Insider's View

One of the most popular segments on the UFC's YouTube channel is the "Embedded" series. These video blogs take fans on a week-long journey leading up to a UFC event. Viewers get an inside look at fighters' training, preparations, and the emotional rollercoaster they experience before stepping into the Octagon.

Fighter Interviews: Unfiltered Conversations

The UFC's YouTube channel also features exclusive fighter interviews. These unfiltered conversations provide insight into fighters' thoughts, strategies, and aspirations. It's a chance for fighters to connect with fans on a personal level and share their perspectives on the sport.

Live Event Coverage: Previews and Post-Fight Analysis

The channel doesn't limit itself to pre-recorded content. UFC events are often accompanied by live streams, where fans can tune in for pre-fight previews, post-fight analysis, and even live weigh-ins. These live segments create a sense of community, allowing fans to interact and discuss the fights in real-time.

UFC Embedded: International Expansion

The UFC's YouTube channel is also a vital tool for expanding its global audience. With multilingual content and subtitles, fans from around the world can enjoy the UFC's offerings. This inclusivity has contributed to the sport's international growth and appeal.

A Digital Powerhouse

The UFC's YouTube channel is not just a platform for sharing fight footage; it's a dynamic digital powerhouse. It brings fans closer to the action, offers unparalleled behind-the-scenes access, and serves as a bridge between fighters and their supporters. In an era where the digital realm is essential for sports promotion, the UFC's YouTube channel stands as a testament to the organization's commitment to providing fans with the ultimate MMA experience.

Chapter 67: Keeping the Octagon Clean - UFC's Partnership with USADA

Maintaining the integrity of mixed martial arts (MMA) is paramount for the Ultimate Fighting Championship (UFC). To ensure a level playing field for all fighters and protect the health and safety of competitors, the UFC has forged a significant partnership with the United States Anti-Doping Agency (USADA). In this chapter, we delve into the collaboration between the UFC and USADA and its impact on the world of professional MMA.

The Role of USADA in UFC

The United States Anti-Doping Agency (USADA) is a non-profit organization tasked with promoting clean and healthy competition by enforcing anti-doping rules for various sports organizations, including the UFC. The partnership between the UFC and USADA began in 2015, marking a significant step in the promotion's commitment to eliminating performance-enhancing drugs (PEDs) and ensuring fair competition.

Comprehensive Drug Testing

Under the UFC-USADA partnership, fighters are subject to one of the most rigorous drug-testing programs in professional sports. The testing is comprehensive and includes both in-competition and out-of-competition testing. This means that fighters can be tested at any time, not just on fight night, to prevent doping throughout their training and competition schedules.

Testing Methods

USADA employs various testing methods to detect prohibited substances. Fighters provide blood and urine samples, which are then analyzed for a wide range of banned substances, including steroids, stimulants, diuretics, and more. The stringent testing procedures are designed to catch even the most sophisticated attempts at cheating.

Education and Prevention

The partnership extends beyond testing. USADA provides educational resources to UFC athletes, helping them understand the rules and consequences of doping violations. This proactive approach aims to prevent doping infractions by ensuring fighters are well-informed about the risks associated with PEDs.

Consequences for Violations

The consequences for doping violations in the UFC are severe. Fighters who test positive for banned substances face suspensions, fines, and a tarnished reputation. Repeat offenders may receive even harsher penalties, including potential career-ending suspensions. This strict stance sends a clear message that doping will not be tolerated in the UFC.

Positive Tests and High-Profile Cases

The UFC-USADA partnership has not been without its share of controversies. High-profile fighters, including former champions like Jon Jones, have faced suspensions and legal troubles due to positive drug tests. These cases have garnered significant media attention and highlighted the UFC's commitment to holding all fighters accountable, regardless of their stature in the sport.

Criticism and Controversies

While the partnership has been effective in catching and penalizing drug cheats, it has also faced criticism. Some fighters and fans have questioned the fairness and consistency of testing, arguing that false positives and inconsistencies in punishments have occurred.

The Ongoing Battle for Clean Sport

Despite challenges and controversies, the UFC's partnership with USADA represents a significant step forward in the pursuit of clean and fair competition in MMA. As the sport continues to grow, so too does the importance of upholding its integrity. Through stringent drug testing and education, the UFC aims to create a level playing field where fighters can showcase their skills without the specter of doping looming overhead.

A Commitment to Clean Competition

The UFC's partnership with the United States Anti-Doping Agency (USADA) is a testament to the organization's commitment to maintaining the integrity of mixed martial arts. By implementing one of the most comprehensive and rigorous drug-testing programs in professional sports, the UFC aims to ensure that fighters compete on a level playing field, free from the influence of performance-enhancing substances. While challenges and controversies may arise, the pursuit of clean and fair competition remains a fundamental principle in the world of the UFC.

Chapter 68: Jon Jones - A Controversial Figure Beyond the Octagon

Jon "Bones" Jones, a name synonymous with MMA excellence, is a fighter whose career is as storied outside the Octagon as it is inside. While celebrated for his undeniable talent and numerous accomplishments, Jones has been no stranger to controversy, legal issues, and personal struggles. In this chapter, we delve into the multifaceted career of Jon Jones and explore the controversies that have marked his journey.

The Rise to Superstardom

Jon Jones burst onto the MMA scene like a meteor, quickly ascending the ranks of the UFC's Light Heavyweight division. His incredible athleticism, unique fighting style, and ability to dominate opponents made him a sensation. Jones won the UFC Light Heavyweight Championship in 2011, becoming the youngest champion in the organization's history.

Early Controversies

Even in his early career, Jones was not immune to controversy. He faced criticism for his flashy, often unorthodox fighting style and was occasionally labeled as disrespectful by opponents. However, these early controversies paled in comparison to what would come later.

Hit-and-Run Incident

One of the most significant controversies involving Jon Jones occurred in April 2015 when he was involved in a hit-and-run incident in Albuquerque, New Mexico. Jones fled the scene of the accident, leaving a pregnant woman with a broken arm. He later turned himself in to the police and faced legal consequences, including probation and community service.

Doping Violations

Jones's career has been marred by multiple doping violations. He tested positive for banned substances, including cocaine and anabolic steroids, on separate occasions. These violations resulted in suspensions and tarnished his reputation. Some critics argue that these incidents raise questions about the fairness of his accomplishments in the Octagon.

Stripped Titles

Due to his legal troubles and doping violations, Jon Jones was stripped of his UFC Light Heavyweight Championship on multiple occasions. These controversies disrupted his reign as the division's dominant force and created uncertainty around his future in the sport.

Personal Struggles

Beyond legal and doping issues, Jones has publicly struggled with personal demons. He has spoken openly about his battles with alcoholism and has sought rehabilitation. These personal challenges have added depth to his public persona, showing that even the most celebrated athletes are not immune to human frailties.

Redemption and Comebacks

Despite his controversies, Jon Jones remains one of the most formidable fighters in MMA history. He has staged remarkable comebacks, recapturing his championship titles and showcasing his incredible skill set. These moments of redemption have endeared him to fans and reminded the world of his undeniable talent.

Ongoing Legacy

Jon Jones's legacy in the world of MMA is a complex one. He is simultaneously celebrated as one of the greatest fighters of all time and criticized for his behavior outside the Octagon. His career serves as a reminder that even the most gifted athletes are not immune to the pitfalls of fame and success. As he continues to compete and seek personal growth, the story of Jon Jones remains one of the most captivating in the sport's history.

A Polarizing Figure

Jon Jones's journey through the world of mixed martial arts is marked by both unparalleled success and significant controversy. His undeniable talent inside the Octagon has earned him a place among the sport's all-time greats. However, his tumultuous personal life and run-ins with the law have made him a polarizing figure. Whether celebrated or criticized, there is no denying the impact Jon Jones has had on the sport of MMA, both for better and for worse.

Chapter 69: A Diverse Spectrum of Martial Arts in the UFC

The UFC has always been a melting pot of martial arts, drawing fighters from a wide spectrum of disciplines. It is this diverse array of backgrounds and skills that has contributed to the UFC's unparalleled popularity and its status as the premier mixed martial arts (MMA) organization in the world. In this chapter, we will explore the rich tapestry of martial arts that find expression in the UFC.

Boxing: The Sweet Science in the Octagon

Boxing, often referred to as "the sweet science," is one of the oldest and most fundamental combat sports. Fighters like Conor McGregor, Anderson Silva, and Max Holloway have showcased their boxing skills in the UFC. Boxing's emphasis on striking, footwork, and head movement has proven invaluable in the Octagon, allowing fighters to land precise punches and evade opponents with finesse.

Kickboxing and Muay Thai: The Art of Eight Limbs

Kickboxing and Muay Thai are striking arts known for their devastating kicks, knee strikes, and clinch work. Fighters such as Jose Aldo, Joanna Jedrzejczyk, and Alistair Overeem have integrated these techniques seamlessly into their MMA arsenals. Muay Thai's clinch work, in particular, has been used to control opponents and deliver powerful strikes.

Brazilian Jiu-Jitsu: The Gentle Art

Brazilian Jiu-Jitsu (BJJ) is renowned for its focus on ground fighting, submissions, and positional control. UFC legends like Royce Gracie, Demian Maia, and the Nogueira brothers, Antonio Rodrigo and Antonio Rogerio, have all demonstrated the effectiveness of BJJ in the Octagon. BJJ practitioners often use leverage and technique to submit opponents or neutralize their attacks, making it a cornerstone of MMA.

Wrestling: The Art of Takedowns and Control

Wrestling is synonymous with takedowns, control, and ground-and-pound. Fighters like Daniel Cormier, Khabib Nurmagomedov, and Randy Couture have showcased their wrestling prowess in the UFC. Wrestling provides the essential skills for dictating where the fight takes place, whether standing or on the ground.

Karate: Striking with Precision

Karate's emphasis on speed and precision in striking has found a home in the UFC. Fighters like Lyoto Machida, Stephen "Wonderboy" Thompson, and Georges St-Pierre have effectively utilized karate-based techniques, including front kicks and sidekicks, to keep opponents at bay and score points in the Octagon.

Capoeira: A Dance of Martial Artistry

Capoeira, an Afro-Brazilian martial art known for its acrobatics and fluid movements, has made occasional appearances in the UFC. Fighters like Edson Barboza have integrated Capoeira kicks and spinning attacks into their striking game, adding an element of surprise and creativity to their fights.

Other Martial Arts: A Constant Evolution

The UFC continually evolves as fighters experiment with new martial arts and techniques. Taekwondo, judo, sambo, and even traditional martial arts like Wing Chun have all made brief appearances, expanding the UFC's diverse martial arts tapestry.

A Dynamic and Evolving Landscape

The UFC's appeal lies not only in its thrilling fights but also in the eclectic blend of martial arts that fighters bring to the Octagon. It is a testament to the evolution of MMA that the most successful fighters are often those who have mastered multiple disciplines. This diversity ensures that every UFC event is a showcase of martial arts at their finest, with fighters drawing from various traditions and backgrounds to create their unique fighting styles. The UFC's success, in no small part, can be attributed to the rich and ever-evolving landscape of martial arts that it represents.

Chapter 70: Conor McGregor - A Meteoric Rise to UFC Stardom

Conor McGregor, often referred to as "The Notorious," is undeniably one of the most iconic and influential figures in the history of the Ultimate Fighting Championship (UFC). His journey from a struggling fighter in Ireland to a global superstar has left an indelible mark on the sport of mixed martial arts (MMA) and played a pivotal role in bringing the UFC into the mainstream.

Early Life and Beginnings

Conor Anthony McGregor was born on July 14, 1988, in Dublin, Ireland. His early life was marked by hardship and a passion for combat sports. McGregor dabbled in various martial arts, including boxing and kickboxing, before eventually finding his way to Brazilian Jiu-Jitsu and MMA.

The Cage Warriors Era

McGregor's first taste of professional MMA came in 2008 when he made his debut with Cage of Truth in Ireland. He swiftly amassed a record of 4-1 and gained attention for his striking prowess and self-confidence. In 2012, he signed with the UK-based promotion Cage Warriors and won the Featherweight and Lightweight titles, becoming a two-division champion.

UFC Debut and Featherweight Dominance

McGregor's UFC journey began on April 6, 2013, when he faced Marcus Brimage in Stockholm, Sweden. He won the fight via knockout in just 67 seconds, setting the tone for what would be an electrifying UFC career. His knockout power, charismatic personality, and memorable trash talk soon made him a fan favorite.

In December 2015, McGregor faced José Aldo for the UFC Featherweight Championship. The fight lasted a mere 13 seconds, with McGregor landing a devastating left hook to claim the title. It was the fastest knockout in a UFC title fight, propelling McGregor into superstardom.

Champion in Two Weight Classes

McGregor's ambitions knew no bounds. He moved up to the Lightweight division and, in November 2016, became the first fighter in UFC history to hold titles in two weight classes simultaneously. He defeated Eddie Alvarez for the UFC Lightweight Championship.

Trash Talk and Entertainment Value

Beyond his fighting skills, McGregor's gift for verbal warfare and showmanship elevated him to another level of fame. His pre-fight antics and press conferences were must-see events, captivating audiences and generating immense interest in his fights.

Crossing Over into Boxing

In 2017, McGregor stepped outside the Octagon and into the world of professional boxing to face the undefeated Floyd Mayweather Jr. Although he lost the bout, the event was one of the biggest pay-per-view spectacles in history, further solidifying McGregor's status as a global sports icon.

Challenges and Comebacks

McGregor's career was not without its challenges. Injuries and outside-the-cage incidents interrupted his fighting momentum. However, he continued to return with a fervor, determined to prove himself.

Impact on the UFC and MMA

Conor McGregor's rise brought unprecedented attention to the UFC and MMA as a whole. His fights shattered pay-per-view records, and his influence extended beyond the sport, with a massive following on social media. McGregor's success paved the way for other fighters to pursue their dreams and find mainstream recognition.

Business Ventures

Outside the cage, McGregor ventured into business, launching his Proper No. Twelve Irish whiskey brand. His business acumen and promotional skills helped him further establish his brand.

Legacy and Future

Conor McGregor's legacy in the UFC is secure, and he remains an enigmatic figure in the world of combat sports. His return to the Octagon after brief retirements has continued to draw massive audiences. While his future in MMA remains uncertain, his impact is undeniable.

A UFC Icon

Conor McGregor's meteoric rise from an aspiring fighter in Ireland to a global superstar transcended the sport of MMA. His charisma, fighting prowess, and larger-than-life persona helped propel the UFC into the mainstream, leaving an indelible mark on the sport's history. Conor McGregor's legacy in the UFC is one of success, controversy, and undeniable star power.

Chapter 71: UFC Across the United States - From Coast to Coast: The American Heartland of MMA

The United States is undoubtedly the birthplace and stronghold of the Ultimate Fighting Championship. Since its inception, the UFC has crisscrossed the country, bringing the excitement of mixed martial arts (MMA) to fans in cities both large and small. In this chapter, we'll explore how the UFC has established a robust presence in cities across the United States.

Las Vegas, Nevada - The UFC's Home Base

While the UFC has traveled far and wide, it's important to acknowledge its home base in Las Vegas, Nevada. Sin City has been the epicenter of the UFC's operations for many years, hosting countless events, including major pay-per-views, press conferences, and fighter training at the UFC Performance Institute. The T-Mobile Arena, in particular, has become synonymous with big UFC fights, including marquee events like UFC 200 and UFC 229.

New York, New York - Legalization and the Madison Square Garden Dream

New York was a long-standing holdout in terms of legalizing MMA. However, in 2016, the state finally sanctioned professional MMA competitions. The UFC seized the opportunity and hosted its first event at the world-famous Madison Square Garden, making history. The venue has since become a favorite for UFC events, hosting some of the most memorable fights in recent years.

Los Angeles, California - Hollywood Meets MMA

California, particularly the Los Angeles area, has been a hub for MMA training and a hotbed for talent. The UFC has regularly brought events to the Golden State, with locations like the Staples Center and The Forum serving as iconic venues. Los Angeles, with its Hollywood connection, has attracted numerous celebrities to UFC events.

Las Vegas, Nevada - The Ultimate Fighter Era

Las Vegas holds another distinction in UFC history as the home of "The Ultimate Fighter" reality TV series. The UFC Apex, a state-of-the-art production facility in Las Vegas, has been instrumental in the filming of the series. Many fighters who emerged from "The Ultimate Fighter" have gone on to become UFC champions and stars.

Atlantic City, New Jersey - East Coast Fights

The UFC hasn't limited itself to the West Coast. Atlantic City, New Jersey, has hosted multiple UFC events, providing a platform for fighters from the East Coast to showcase their skills. The city's historic Boardwalk Hall and Revel Casino have witnessed memorable Octagon battles.

Chicago, Illinois - The Windy City's MMA Love

Chicago has been a welcoming city for the UFC, with venues like the United Center hosting events. The UFC's Windy City presence has allowed fans in the Midwest to experience the thrill of live MMA action.

Boston, Massachusetts - A Historic Return

Boston, home to some of the nation's oldest sports traditions, has embraced the UFC. The TD Garden has been the site of several UFC events, including the return of MMA to Massachusetts after its legalization.

The American Landscape of UFC

The United States serves as the backbone of the UFC, providing a diverse array of cities and venues for the promotion to showcase its fights. From the bright lights of Las Vegas to the historic halls of Madison Square Garden and arenas across the nation, the UFC's presence in the United States continues to thrive. This extensive reach ensures that fans from coast to coast can witness the excitement and drama of the Octagon, solidifying the UFC's status as a quintessential American sport.

Chapter 72: The Thrilling World of UFC Fight Night Events - Where Every Bout Matters

The UFC Fight Night series has become an integral part of the mixed martial arts (MMA) landscape. These events, often held on a regular basis, offer fans the chance to witness exhilarating matchups, rising stars, and established veterans in action. In this chapter, we'll delve into the exciting world of UFC Fight Night events and explore what makes them a unique and essential part of the UFC experience.

The Evolution of Fight Nights

UFC Fight Nights have come a long way since their inception. Originally conceived as a platform to showcase up-and-coming talent, these events have evolved into something much more significant. While they still serve as a proving ground for emerging fighters, they now also feature marquee matchups, former champions looking for redemption, and established contenders vying for title shots.

Global Reach

One of the defining features of UFC Fight Night events is their global reach. The UFC's commitment to expanding its brand worldwide is reflected in these events being held in various countries and cities. From Las Vegas to London, São Paulo to Seoul, Fight Nights give MMA fans across the globe the opportunity to witness live action.

Main Event Showcases

While Fight Nights may not always have title fights as their main events, they regularly feature high-stakes bouts that captivate fans. These main events often serve as a stepping stone for fighters to ascend the rankings and earn title opportunities. The competitive nature of these contests ensures that every Fight Night is filled with suspense and excitement.

Opportunities for Rising Stars

UFC Fight Nights are a breeding ground for the UFC's next generation of stars. Talented fighters from regional promotions or "The Ultimate Fighter" reality show are given the chance to shine on a bigger stage. Many of today's UFC champions and fan favorites made their marks during Fight Night events, proving that anyone can become a household name in the MMA world.

Fight of the Night and Performance Bonuses

Fight Night events frequently produce memorable battles that are awarded the coveted "Fight of the Night" bonuses. These bonuses not only recognize exceptional performances but also provide fighters with financial incentives. "Performance of the Night" bonuses further encourage fighters to push their limits and deliver thrilling moments.

Fan Engagement and Accessibility

The UFC's commitment to fan engagement is evident during Fight Night events. These shows often feature Q&A sessions, open workouts, and meet-and-greets with fighters, allowing fans to interact with their MMA idols. Additionally, the accessibility of Fight Nights, both in terms of ticket prices and television broadcasts, makes them an attractive option for fans of all backgrounds.

The Heartbeat of UFC

UFC Fight Night events embody the essence of mixed martial arts: determination, passion, and the pursuit of greatness. They provide a platform for fighters to showcase their skills and tell their stories. These events have not only contributed to the growth of the sport but have also enriched the lives of countless fans who eagerly anticipate the next Fight Night showdown. As the UFC continues to expand its reach, Fight Nights remain an essential and thrilling component of the world of MMA.

Chapter 73: Unconventional Training Methods in the World of UFC

When it comes to preparing for the Octagon, UFC fighters are known for their dedication and innovation. While conventional training methods like sparring and strength conditioning remain essential, many fighters have adopted unique and unconventional approaches to gain an edge in the world of mixed martial arts. In this chapter, we'll explore some of the intriguing and unconventional training methods employed by UFC athletes.

High-Altitude Training: Gaining an Oxygen Advantage

Training at high altitudes, typically above 7,000 feet (2,100 meters), has become a popular strategy among UFC fighters. The thin air at high altitudes forces the body to adapt by producing more red blood cells and improving oxygen utilization. This adaptation can enhance an athlete's endurance, a crucial factor in MMA where fights can go the distance.

One of the most famous advocates of high-altitude training is former UFC Lightweight Champion Khabib Nurmagomedov. He often trained in the mountains of his native Dagestan, where the elevation exceeds 14,000 feet (4,300 meters). The results were evident in his seemingly endless gas tank during fights.

Cross-Training in Unrelated Disciplines: A Well-Rounded Approach

While many UFC fighters come from specific martial arts backgrounds like Brazilian Jiu-Jitsu or Muay Thai, some have taken cross-training to the next level by incorporating entirely unrelated disciplines into their routines.

For instance, former UFC Women's Bantamweight Champion Ronda Rousey used judo techniques extensively in her MMA career, thanks to her Olympic-level background in the sport. Her ability to seamlessly integrate judo throws into her fights made her a dominant force in the Octagon.

Specialized Coaching: Seeking Expertise

Fighters often seek out specialized coaches to gain an edge in particular aspects of their game. This can include working with Olympic-level wrestlers, world-class boxers, or renowned Brazilian Jiu-Jitsu black belts. These specialists provide invaluable insights and training regimens that can take a fighter's skills to new heights.

Cognitive Training: Sharpening the Mind

In the fast-paced world of MMA, mental acuity is as crucial as physical prowess. Some fighters have turned to cognitive training methods to improve their focus, reaction times, and decision-making under pressure. Techniques such as neurofeedback, meditation, and visualization have been employed to gain a mental edge inside the Octagon.

Unique Sparring Partners: Mimicking Opponents

To prepare for specific opponents, fighters often bring in training partners who can replicate their adversaries' fighting styles. This includes finding individuals with similar body types, striking techniques, or grappling skills. This meticulous approach allows fighters to develop strategies tailored to their upcoming challenges.

The Quest for the Edge

UFC fighters are a diverse and innovative group, constantly seeking new methods to gain a competitive edge. Whether it's training at high altitudes to boost endurance or embracing unconventional training partners and coaching, these athletes are willing to go to great lengths to excel in the Octagon. As the sport continues to evolve, we can expect even more unique and inventive training methods to emerge, pushing the boundaries of what's possible in mixed martial arts.

Chapter 74: Fighter Safety and the Dedicated Medical Staff of the UFC

In the high-octane world of the UFC, fighter safety is paramount. The physical demands and risks associated with mixed martial arts are considerable, and the UFC takes extensive measures to protect its athletes. At the forefront of these efforts is the dedicated medical staff that plays a crucial role in ensuring the well-being of fighters. In this chapter, we delve into the comprehensive medical support system that the UFC has in place.

Fight Week Medical Examinations: A Thorough Start

Fighters participating in UFC events undergo a series of medical examinations well before they step into the Octagon. Fight week begins with rigorous medical assessments to ensure that competitors are in good health and fit to compete. These examinations include comprehensive physicals, blood work, neurological evaluations, and vision tests.

The Role of Ringside Physicians: Experts at the Ready

During UFC events, a team of experienced ringside physicians is present to provide immediate medical attention if needed. These physicians are highly trained in combat sports medicine and are prepared to step in at a moment's notice to assess injuries and make critical decisions regarding fighter safety.

Medical Suspensions: Protecting Fighters From Themselves

In the aftermath of a fight, the medical staff plays a pivotal role in determining when fighters are fit to return to action. Fighters who have sustained injuries or shown signs of neurological impairment may be placed on medical suspension. This precautionary measure is designed to protect fighters from themselves, ensuring they have adequate time to recover before engaging in further competition.

Concussion Protocols: Prioritizing Brain Health

Concussions are a serious concern in combat sports, and the UFC takes them very seriously. The medical staff follows stringent concussion protocols, which include a battery of tests to evaluate a fighter's cognitive function. If a fighter is suspected of having suffered a concussion, they are immediately removed from competition and subject to a mandatory rest period.

Emergency Medical Services: Prepared for Any Scenario

In the rare event of a severe injury or medical emergency inside the Octagon, the UFC has a contingency plan in place. Emergency medical services, including paramedics and ambulances, are on standby at every event. These trained professionals are ready to respond swiftly to any critical situation, ensuring that fighters receive immediate care.

Post-Fight Medical Evaluations: Assessing Damage

After the dust settles and the roar of the crowd subsides, fighters undergo thorough post-fight medical evaluations. This includes examinations of any injuries sustained during the fight, ensuring that fighters receive appropriate medical attention before they leave the venue.

The UFC PI: A Resource for Fighter Rehabilitation

The UFC Performance Institute (PI) in Las Vegas also plays a role in fighter safety. Injured fighters can turn to the PI for rehabilitation services and support during their recovery journey. The facility offers state-of-the-art equipment and a team of experts to help fighters get back to peak condition safely.

A Comprehensive Safety Net

The UFC's commitment to fighter safety is unwavering. The dedicated medical staff, along with stringent pre-fight and post-fight protocols, ensures that fighters are well-protected throughout their careers. This comprehensive approach not only safeguards the health of UFC athletes but also sets a standard for safety in the world of combat sports.

Chapter 75: The Marquee Attractions - UFC Championship Bouts

In the world of mixed martial arts, nothing quite captures the imagination of fans and fighters alike like a UFC championship bout. These contests are the pinnacle of the sport, where warriors step into the Octagon with the ultimate prize on the line - a UFC championship belt. In this chapter, we delve into the significance and spectacle of UFC championship bouts that often serve as the main event of UFC events.

The Coveted Titles: A Symbol of Excellence

UFC championships represent the zenith of achievement in MMA. They are the tangible symbol of a fighter's dedication, skill, and dominance in their respective weight classes. Each division has its own championship belt, and these belts are often the focal point of fighters' careers. Winning one is a dream come true for any mixed martial artist.

The Five-Round Standard: Championship Fight Duration

UFC championship bouts are unique in that they are scheduled for five rounds, unlike regular fights, which are typically three rounds. This additional time not only tests a fighter's physical prowess but also their mental and emotional fortitude. Championship rounds have witnessed some of the sport's most iconic moments, where fighters push themselves to the limit.

Championship Fight Atmosphere: The Crowd Roars

When a UFC championship bout is announced as the main event, the atmosphere becomes electric. Fans from around the world tune in to witness history in the making. The arenas are filled to capacity, and the crowd's energy is palpable. The walkout songs, the fighter introductions, and the stare-downs all add to the tension and excitement.

Memorable Moments: Legendary Title Fights

Throughout UFC history, championship bouts have produced unforgettable moments. Fighters like Anderson Silva, Georges St-Pierre, Jon Jones, and Amanda Nunes have etched their names into MMA lore with their championship performances. From thrilling knockouts to dramatic comebacks, these fights have left an indelible mark on the sport.

The Challenger's Journey: The Path to Glory

Challengers in UFC championship bouts often face a grueling journey to earn their shot at the title. They must climb the rankings, defeat elite opponents, and prove themselves as the most deserving contenders. This journey is a testament to their resilience and determination.

Title Changes and Legacies: The Dynamic Nature of MMA

The landscape of the UFC is ever-evolving, and championship titles change hands. This dynamism keeps the sport fresh and unpredictable. Fighters like Conor McGregor, who held two titles simultaneously, and Amanda Nunes, who has dominated multiple divisions, have redefined what it means to be a champion.

UFC championship bouts are the epitome of mixed martial arts excellence. They represent the culmination of years of hard work, sacrifice, and dedication for fighters. As these athletes step into the Octagon with the world watching, they carry the weight of history on their shoulders, and their performances in championship bouts are etched into the annals of MMA greatness.

Chapter 76: Neil Magny's Remarkable Journey from the Military to the Octagon

Neil Magny's journey to becoming a successful UFC fighter is nothing short of remarkable. Before stepping into the Octagon, he wore a different uniform and served his country in the United States Army National Guard. His story is a testament to dedication, perseverance, and the ability to balance two vastly different worlds – military service and a career in mixed martial arts (MMA).

Early Life and Military Service

Neil Magny was born on August 3, 1987, in Brooklyn, New York. He grew up in a supportive family, and like many young individuals, he had dreams and aspirations. Neil's path, however, took a unique turn when he made the decision to serve his country. He joined the United States Army National Guard, a branch of the military that combines part-time service with civilian life.

During his time in the National Guard, Neil Magny learned valuable life skills, including discipline, leadership, and time management. These qualities would later prove crucial in his MMA career. Serving in the military provided him with a strong foundation and instilled in him the values of hard work and determination.

The Transition to Mixed Martial Arts

While still serving in the National Guard, Neil Magny discovered a passion for mixed martial arts. It was during this time that he began training in various disciplines, including Brazilian Jiu-Jitsu and wrestling. His natural athleticism and dedication quickly became evident, and he showed significant promise as a fighter.

Balancing his military obligations with his MMA training was no easy feat. Neil had to manage his time meticulously, often training late into the night after fulfilling his military duties. It was a grueling schedule, but he persevered, driven by his desire to pursue a career in the UFC.

UFC Debut and Rise to Prominence

In 2012, Neil Magny made his UFC debut, marking the beginning of his professional MMA career. His debut fight was against Jon Manley at The Ultimate Fighter 16 Finale. Although he faced adversity in his early UFC bouts, Magny's determination and continuous improvement were evident.

One of the defining moments of Neil Magny's career came when he participated in multiple fights in a single year, earning him the nickname "The Leech" due to his relentless fighting style. This level of activity was rare in the UFC and showcased his unwavering commitment to the sport.

Overcoming Challenges

Neil Magny's journey in the UFC was not without its challenges. He faced tough opponents and experienced both victories and defeats. However, his resilience and ability to learn from each fight allowed him to steadily climb the welterweight rankings.

One of the key factors contributing to his success was the discipline he had cultivated during his time in the military. Neil Magny's military background taught him the importance of preparation, mental toughness, and never giving up, qualities that served him well in the Octagon.

Continuing to Inspire

Neil Magny's story continues to inspire many, both in the military and the world of MMA. His remarkable journey from serving in the United States Army National Guard to becoming a respected UFC fighter demonstrates that with determination and hard work, one can achieve their dreams even in the face of adversity.

As he continues to compete in the UFC, Neil Magny remains a symbol of dedication, resilience, and the unwavering pursuit of excellence, proving that a strong work ethic and the ability to overcome challenges can lead to success both inside and outside the Octagon.

Chapter 77: The Power of Connection - Fighters and Their Social Media Presence

In today's digital age, the world has become more connected than ever, and social media platforms have played a pivotal role in bridging the gap between fighters and their fans. Fighters, whether they are established champions or rising stars, have embraced social media as a means of engaging with their audience, building their personal brand, and promoting upcoming fights.

The Rise of Social Media in MMA

The use of social media by fighters has significantly changed the landscape of mixed martial arts (MMA). It has allowed fans to connect with their favorite fighters on a personal level, gain insights into their training routines, and even participate in Q&A sessions. This direct line of communication has created a sense of intimacy and accessibility that was previously unimaginable.

Platforms like Twitter, Instagram, Facebook, and YouTube have become essential tools for fighters to share their journeys, thoughts, and experiences with a global audience. These platforms enable fighters to showcase their personalities beyond the confines of the Octagon, building loyal fan bases along the way.

Building Personal Brands

Fighters are not just athletes; they are brands in themselves. Social media has provided them with a unique opportunity to shape and cultivate their personal brands. Through carefully curated content, fighters can project their image, values, and aspirations to the world.

Many fighters use their social media accounts to document their daily lives, training camps, and interactions with fellow fighters. These behind-the-scenes glimpses offer fans a more authentic and unfiltered view of their favorite athletes. Additionally, fighters often share their interests, hobbies, and philanthropic efforts, humanizing them in the eyes of their fans.

Interactions with Fans

One of the most significant benefits of social media for fighters is the ability to interact directly with their fans. Whether it's responding to comments, hosting live Q&A sessions, or sharing fan-created artwork, fighters can make their followers feel valued and appreciated. This engagement fosters a sense of community and strengthens the bond between fighters and their fan base.

Fighters also use social media to provide updates on their training progress, injury recoveries, and fight preparations. This real-time connection allows fans to stay informed and emotionally invested in their fighter's journey.

Promotion and Fight Hype

Social media is a powerful promotional tool for fighters and promotions like the UFC. Fighters often use platforms like Twitter and Instagram to engage in friendly banter with opponents, creating anticipation and excitement for upcoming bouts. This online rivalry can generate substantial interest and pay-per-view buys for events.

The UFC itself uses social media to announce fights, share highlights, and provide exclusive content to its fans. Fighters frequently participate in promotional campaigns, such as countdown videos and face-offs, to build hype around their fights.

The Dark Side of Social Media

While social media has brought numerous advantages to fighters, it also has a dark side. Fighters can face online harassment, negativity, and unwarranted criticism from trolls and detractors. Some fighters have had to take breaks from social media to protect their mental well-being. It's a reminder that, despite the benefits, social media can also be a challenging space.

The relationship between fighters and social media is symbiotic. Fighters gain visibility, engagement, and a direct line of communication with their fans, while fans enjoy unparalleled access to their favorite athletes. As social media continues to evolve, its role in the world of MMA will likely grow, further shaping the sport and the way fans connect with the fighters they admire. In this era of digital connection, social media has become an integral part of the MMA experience, enriching the lives of fighters and fans alike.

Chapter 78: The UFC's Iconic Venue - Madison Square Garden

Madison Square Garden, often referred to simply as "The Garden," is one of the most iconic sporting and entertainment venues in the world. Located in the heart of Manhattan, New York City, this historic arena has played host to some of the most significant moments in sports and entertainment history. For the UFC, securing Madison Square Garden as a venue was a landmark achievement and a testament to the sport's growing popularity.

A Legendary Arena

Madison Square Garden has a rich and storied history dating back to its opening in 1968. It has been the home of countless legendary sporting events, including boxing matches featuring Muhammad Ali, Joe Frazier, and Mike Tyson. The arena has also been a stage for music icons like Elvis Presley and The Rolling Stones.

The Garden's central location in Manhattan makes it a cultural and entertainment hub, attracting fans and spectators from all over the world. It boasts a seating capacity of over 20,000 for combat sports events, creating an electric atmosphere that is unrivaled.

UFC's Journey to Madison Square Garden

For many years, the UFC faced legal and regulatory hurdles that prevented it from hosting events in the state of New York. The prohibition on professional MMA in New York was a contentious issue, with supporters arguing for its economic benefits and detractors concerned about safety and regulation.

However, in 2016, after years of lobbying and legal battles, the New York State Assembly finally voted to legalize professional MMA, opening the door for the UFC to host events in the state. This historic decision allowed the UFC to make its long-awaited debut at Madison Square Garden.

UFC 205: A Landmark Event

On November 12, 2016, the UFC made its Madison Square Garden debut with UFC 205. This event was historic for several reasons. It marked the first time the UFC had been granted a license to host professional MMA fights in New York, and it was the first MMA event ever held at Madison Square Garden.

The fight card for UFC 205 was stacked with star power. The main event featured Eddie Alvarez defending his lightweight title against Conor McGregor, who aimed to become the first fighter in UFC history to hold titles in two weight classes simultaneously. McGregor made history by winning the lightweight title, adding another layer of significance to the event.

Legacy and Future

Since UFC 205, Madison Square Garden has continued to be a premier venue for the UFC. The promotion has returned to The Garden multiple times, solidifying its status as a marquee destination for MMA fans.

Madison Square Garden represents more than just a venue; it symbolizes the UFC's growth and acceptance as a mainstream sport. It's a place where fighters strive to etch their names in the annals of MMA history, and where fans come to witness history being made.

Madison Square Garden's association with the UFC is a testament to the sport's journey from the fringes to the mainstream. It stands as an iconic venue where champions are crowned, legends are born, and unforgettable moments unfold, forever etching the UFC's place in the rich tapestry of Madison Square Garden's history.

Chapter 79: The UFC Hall of Fame Induction Ceremony

The UFC Hall of Fame, a place of honor and recognition, stands as a testament to the incredible journeys and contributions made by fighters, coaches, and other key figures in the world of mixed martial arts. Established in 2003 at UFC 45, this hall of fame has grown over the years, celebrating excellence and the remarkable legacy of those who have left an indelible mark on the sport.

Inaugural Class of Legends

The UFC Hall of Fame began with a bang, as the inaugural class featured some of the true pioneers and legends of mixed martial arts. These individuals, including the likes of Royce Gracie, Ken Shamrock, and Dan Severn, were instrumental in shaping the early days of the UFC. Their dedication and groundbreaking performances helped transform MMA into the global phenomenon it is today.

Categories of Recognition

The UFC Hall of Fame doesn't just celebrate fighters; it also recognizes those who have contributed to the sport in various ways. It features several categories:

1. **Modern-era Wing:** This category pays homage to fighters, both male and female, who have achieved remarkable success in the

modern era of the UFC. These are individuals who have held championship titles and showcased extraordinary skills.
2. **Pioneer Wing:** The pioneers of the sport, a fitting category name, are those who laid the foundation for MMA and the UFC. They were the ones who established the sport's credibility and deserve recognition for their contributions.
3. **Contributors Wing:** MMA is a collective effort, involving many behind-the-scenes individuals. The Contributors Wing acknowledges referees, judges, coaches, and executives who have played pivotal roles in the sport's growth and development.
4. **Fight Wing:** Some fights in UFC history are so iconic and memorable that they deserve a category of their own. The Fight Wing celebrates these legendary battles that have left a lasting impact on the sport.

Annual Induction Ceremony

Each year, the UFC holds an induction ceremony to honor the new Hall of Fame inductees. These ceremonies take place during UFC International Fight Week, an annual event that brings together fighters, fans, and the entire MMA community. It's a special occasion where past and present collide, and the UFC family comes together to celebrate the sport's rich history.

The Legends Among Us

The list of UFC Hall of Famers reads like a who's who of mixed martial arts. Fighters like Chuck Liddell, Matt Hughes, and Forrest Griffin have found their place in the Modern-era Wing. Pioneers like Mark Coleman and contributors like Bruce Buffer have received well-deserved recognition.

A Symbol of Legacy

The UFC Hall of Fame serves as a reminder of the incredible journey the sport of MMA has undertaken. It's a testament to the blood, sweat, and tears shed by fighters inside the Octagon and the unwavering dedication of those who have nurtured the sport from the outside.

Honoring the Past, Inspiring the Future

In the world of mixed martial arts, the UFC Hall of Fame is the pinnacle of recognition, a place where legends are immortalized, and their legacies live on. It's a symbol of the sport's evolution and a tribute to those who have helped it become the global phenomenon it is today. As the UFC continues to grow, so too will the Hall of Fame, ensuring that the stories of its most remarkable individuals are never forgotten.

Chapter 80: Fighters from Different Generations in the UFC - Early Days vs. Modern Era

The UFC, throughout its storied history, has witnessed fighters from different generations stepping into the Octagon. This clash of eras often leads to intriguing matchups and debates among fans and experts alike.

Pioneers of the Sport

In the early days of the UFC, fighters like Royce Gracie, Ken Shamrock, and Dan Severn were among the pioneers of mixed martial arts. These legends competed when the sport was still in its infancy, and the rules were relatively lax compared to today's standards.

Evolution of Techniques

As the sport evolved, so did the techniques and strategies employed by fighters. The early generation of fighters relied heavily on their expertise in one discipline, be it Brazilian Jiu-Jitsu or wrestling. These pioneers paved the way for future generations to develop well-rounded skills.

Cross-Generational Fights

One fascinating aspect of the UFC is the occasional cross-generational fight. These matchups pit a seasoned veteran against a rising star or another fighter from a different era. Such fights provide a unique opportunity to see how the sport has progressed over time.

Anderson Silva vs. Israel Adesanya

A perfect example of a cross-generational fight was the showdown between Anderson Silva, a middleweight legend, and Israel Adesanya, a rising star known for his striking prowess. Silva, who had dominated the middleweight division in his prime, faced Adesanya, who had adopted some of Silva's own striking techniques. The fight was a testament to the evolution of striking in MMA.

The Debate of GOATs

The clash of generations often sparks discussions about the Greatest of All Time (GOAT) in MMA. Fans and experts debate whether fighters from the early days could compete with modern champions, and vice versa. This debate adds an extra layer of excitement to these cross-generational matchups.

Legacy and Evolution

The UFC's ability to host fights between fighters from different generations showcases the sport's evolution. It's a testament to the dedication and talent of athletes who have propelled MMA from its humble beginnings to the global phenomenon it is today. These cross-generational clashes serve as a reminder of the sport's rich history and its promising future.

Chapter 81: Fighter Pre-Fight Rituals

Before they step into the Octagon, fighters often have unique rituals and routines to prepare both mentally and physically. These pre-fight rituals can vary significantly from one fighter to another, reflecting their individual personalities and superstitions.

Visualization and Shadowboxing

Many fighters find solace in visualizing their upcoming bout. They close their eyes and run through various scenarios in their minds, imagining themselves executing their fight strategy flawlessly. Visualization helps fighters build confidence and mentally prepare for the battle ahead.

Shadowboxing is another common pre-fight ritual. Fighters use this time to warm up their muscles, sharpen their striking, and focus their minds. It's a way to get into the flow of the fight, and some fighters even perform it in their locker rooms just minutes before entering the Octagon.

Music Selection

The choice of walkout music is a significant aspect of a fighter's pre-fight ritual. This music sets the tone for the entrance and can reflect the fighter's personality or cultural background. Some fighters opt for high-energy tracks to pump themselves up, while others choose more calming tunes to keep their nerves in check.

Meditation and Breathing Exercises

To manage pre-fight jitters and stay calm under pressure, many fighters practice meditation and deep breathing exercises. These techniques help reduce anxiety and promote focus. Controlled breathing can also be used between rounds to recover and maintain composure.

Prayer and Superstitions

For some fighters, pre-fight rituals involve prayer or superstitions. They may have a specific routine of saying a prayer or making the sign of the cross before entering the Octagon. Others wear lucky charms or follow routines they believe bring them good fortune.

Team Huddles

Fighters often gather with their coaches and training partners for a final pep talk and strategy discussion. This huddle serves to boost morale, reinforce the game plan, and provide emotional support. It's a moment of unity before stepping into solo combat.

The War Paint

Some fighters paint their bodies with symbols or messages before a fight. This ritual serves as a visual representation of their mindset and intentions. It can be intimidating to opponents and empowering for the fighters themselves.

Final Thoughts

Fighters' pre-fight rituals are as diverse as the fighters themselves. From visualization to superstitions, each ritual serves a specific purpose in helping fighters prepare for the physical and mental challenges of an MMA bout. These rituals are a fascinating glimpse into the psyche of those who step into the Octagon, showcasing their dedication and commitment to their craft.

Chapter 82: UFC's Social Media Dominance

The Ultimate Fighting Championship (UFC) has embraced the digital age with open arms, establishing a powerful presence on various social media platforms. This strategy has allowed the UFC to connect with fans, share content, and promote its fighters and events in unprecedented ways.

Facebook: A Hub for Fans

With millions of followers on Facebook, the UFC has a massive presence on this popular social media platform. The organization regularly shares fight highlights, event updates, and behind-the-scenes footage. Fans can engage with the content by liking, sharing, and commenting on posts, fostering a sense of community among UFC enthusiasts.

Twitter: Real-Time Updates

Twitter is the go-to platform for real-time updates in the fast-paced world of MMA. The UFC's Twitter account provides live updates during events, including round-by-round commentary and instant reactions to fight outcomes. This platform also serves as a hub for breaking news, fighter callouts, and promotional announcements.

Instagram: Visual Storytelling

UFC's Instagram account focuses on visual storytelling, offering fans an inside look at fighters' lives. From training sessions to personal moments, Instagram allows fighters to connect with their fans on a more personal level. The platform is also home to stunning fight night photography and highlights, making it a visual feast for fight enthusiasts.

YouTube: The Home of Fight Content

YouTube is where the UFC houses an extensive library of fight-related content. Fans can watch full fight replays, event previews, fighter interviews, and more. The UFC's official YouTube channel has become a one-stop-shop for fans looking to dive deep into the world of mixed martial arts.

TikTok: Short-Form Entertainment

TikTok, known for its short-form videos, has also become a platform of choice for the UFC. Here, the organization shares bite-sized highlights, funny fighter moments, and engaging challenges that resonate with a younger audience. It's a fun and creative way to showcase the lighter side of the sport.

Snapchat: Behind-the-Scenes Access

Snapchat allows the UFC to provide fans with exclusive behind-the-scenes access. Fighters take over the UFC's Snapchat account, giving followers a glimpse into their lives leading up to fight night. This platform offers a more intimate and unfiltered perspective on the fighters and the organization.

LinkedIn: Professional Engagement

LinkedIn might not be the first platform that comes to mind for sports organizations, but the UFC utilizes it for professional networking, job postings, and business updates. It's a platform that caters to the UFC's business side, connecting with sponsors, partners, and potential employees.

Reddit: The Fan Community

The UFC also has a presence on Reddit, a platform known for its passionate and engaged communities. Here, fans can discuss fights, share opinions, and interact with fighters and UFC personnel in a more direct way. Reddit serves as an invaluable forum for in-depth MMA discussions.

Future of UFC's Social Media

As technology and social media platforms evolve, the UFC's presence in the digital realm is likely to continue growing. The organization's ability to engage with fans, provide content, and build a global community of MMA enthusiasts remains a cornerstone of its success. UFC's social media dominance not only enhances fan experiences but also plays a pivotal role in promoting the sport of mixed martial arts to a worldwide audience.

Chapter 83: Fighters' Post-Fight Conduct

In the intense world of mixed martial arts (MMA), emotions run high, and fighters often face tremendous pressure. After a fight, their reactions can be as diverse as their fighting styles. While many athletes display professionalism and sportsmanship, some have faced criticism for their post-fight conduct. This chapter delves into various instances where fighters' behavior outside the cage generated headlines and controversy.

Partying and Excessive Celebrations

After a hard-fought victory, it's understandable that fighters want to celebrate. However, some have faced criticism for their excessive partying and celebrations, especially when it negatively affects their training or public image. Fighters like Jon Jones and Conor McGregor have faced backlash for their post-fight partying, which occasionally led to legal issues.

Trash Talking and Feuds

Verbal warfare is an integral part of MMA promotion, but it doesn't always end with the final bell. Some fighters continue to engage in trash talking and feuds well after a fight has concluded. While this can generate interest and pay-per-view buys, it can also cross the line into disrespect and unprofessional behavior. Notable examples include the long-standing feud between Chael Sonnen and Anderson Silva.

Refusal to Shake Hands

Traditionally, fighters are expected to shake hands and show respect to their opponents after a fight, win or lose. However, there have been instances where fighters refused to do so, displaying a lack of sportsmanship. This conduct is usually met with disapproval from fans and fellow fighters alike.

Failed Drug Tests

Perhaps one of the most significant post-fight controversies in MMA is fighters testing positive for banned substances. These instances tarnish not only the fighter's reputation but also the sport's integrity. Fighters like Anderson Silva and Brock Lesnar have faced suspensions and criticism for failing drug tests after their fights.

Unsportsmanlike Behavior Inside the Cage

While post-fight conduct primarily refers to actions outside the cage, some fighters have displayed unsportsmanlike behavior inside it. This includes taunting opponents, illegal strikes, and even late hits after the fight has been stopped. Such behavior can lead to fines, suspensions, and damage to a fighter's image.

Social Media Rants

In the age of social media, fighters often take to platforms like Twitter and Instagram to express themselves. Some have faced backlash for controversial posts or rants targeting opponents, officials, or the promotion itself. These online outbursts can result in consequences both professionally and personally.

While MMA fighters are known for their resilience and determination inside the cage, their post-fight conduct can sometimes overshadow their in-cage accomplishments. Fighters face scrutiny not only for their performance but also for their behavior and actions outside the octagon. It serves as a reminder of the importance of professionalism and sportsmanship in the world of mixed martial arts.

Chapter 84: The Evolution of UFC Weight Classes

The UFC has seen significant growth and evolution in its weight classes over the years. In this chapter, we will explore how the organization's weight divisions have changed and expanded to accommodate fighters of all sizes, contributing to the sport's inclusivity and excitement.

Early Days of Limited Weight Classes

When the UFC was founded in 1993, it had very few weight classes. In fact, the first several UFC events featured an open-weight format, where fighters of vastly different sizes could compete against each other. While this created some memorable matchups, it also raised concerns about fighter safety and fairness.

The Introduction of Weight Classes

Recognizing the need for structure and safety, the UFC introduced its first weight classes in 1997. These initial divisions included Heavyweight, Light Heavyweight, Middleweight, Welterweight, and Lightweight. This marked a significant step towards organizing the talent pool and creating more competitive matchups.

Expansion of Weight Classes

As the sport grew in popularity, the UFC continued to expand its range of weight classes. In 2001, the Featherweight and Bantamweight divisions were introduced, further diversifying the roster and providing opportunities for smaller fighters to showcase their skills.

Women's Weight Classes

The inclusion of women's divisions in 2013 marked another pivotal moment in the UFC's history. The organization introduced the Strawweight and Bantamweight divisions for female fighters. This move opened doors for female fighters like Ronda Rousey, who went on to become one of the most iconic figures in MMA.

The Latest Addition: Flyweight

In 2012, the Flyweight division was introduced for male fighters, further solidifying the UFC's commitment to providing weight classes for athletes of all sizes. This division has seen fierce competition and produced standout champions like Demetrious "Mighty Mouse" Johnson.

A More Inclusive and Competitive UFC

The evolution and expansion of UFC weight classes have transformed the organization into a more inclusive and competitive platform for fighters. Fighters now have more opportunities to compete in divisions that align with their natural weight, reducing the health risks associated with extreme weight cutting.

The evolution of UFC weight classes reflects the organization's commitment to the safety and fairness of the sport while also providing fans with a diverse array of exciting matchups. This expansion has allowed fighters from various weight categories to shine and has contributed to the UFC's status as a global phenomenon in combat sports.

Chapter 85: Unique Training Methods in the UFC

High-Altitude Training

High-altitude training has gained popularity among UFC fighters seeking to gain a competitive edge. Training at high altitudes, typically above 6,000 feet (1,800 meters) above sea level, presents a unique set of challenges and benefits.

- **Altitude Simulation:** Some fighters choose to live and train at high altitudes, such as in locations like Denver, Colorado. The reduced oxygen levels force their bodies to produce more red blood cells to carry oxygen, potentially enhancing their endurance and stamina. When they return to lower altitudes to compete, they may experience improved oxygen utilization.
- **Altitude Masks:** Altitude training masks simulate high-altitude conditions by restricting airflow. Fighters wear these masks during workouts to make their respiratory muscles work harder, potentially improving lung capacity and overall conditioning.
- **Training Camps in High-Altitude Locations:** Several UFC fighters and camps have chosen to host training camps in high-altitude locations, even if their home base is at sea level. This strategic decision is made to adapt to reduced oxygen levels and potentially

gain an advantage when fighting opponents who have not acclimated to the altitude.
- **Benefits and Controversy:** While high-altitude training can offer benefits, including increased red blood cell production and better cardiovascular conditioning, it's not without controversy. Some experts argue that the benefits may be overstated, and the risks of overtraining and burnout are real.

Strength and Conditioning

Strength and conditioning play a vital role in a fighter's performance, and UFC athletes employ various unique methods to enhance their physical attributes.

- **Olympic Weightlifting:** Many fighters incorporate Olympic weightlifting techniques into their training routines. Movements like the clean and jerk and snatch can improve power, explosiveness, and overall strength.
- **Functional Training:** Functional training focuses on exercises that mimic the movements and demands of MMA competition. These workouts can improve a fighter's agility, balance, and coordination.
- **Circuit Training:** Fighters often engage in high-intensity circuit training sessions that combine strength and cardiovascular exercises. These workouts improve overall fitness while simulating the physical demands of a fight.

Mental Preparation

Training the mind is just as crucial as training the body in the UFC. Many fighters use unique mental preparation techniques to stay focused and perform at their best.

- **Visualization:** Visualization involves mentally rehearsing a fight, imagining every detail, from entering the octagon to executing techniques. This technique can enhance confidence and reduce anxiety.
- **Meditation and Mindfulness:** Mindfulness and meditation help fighters manage stress, stay calm under pressure, and maintain mental clarity. These practices are especially useful during fight week.
- **Sports Psychology:** Some fighters work with sports psychologists to develop mental toughness, set goals, and manage performance anxiety. These professionals provide valuable tools to stay mentally resilient.

Nutritional Strategies

Nutrition is a critical aspect of a fighter's training regimen. Some fighters adopt unique dietary strategies to optimize their performance.

- **Intermittent Fasting:** Intermittent fasting involves cycling between periods of fasting and eating. Some fighters believe it can help with weight management and energy utilization.

- **Ketogenic Diet:** The ketogenic diet is low in carbohydrates and high in fats. Some fighters use this diet to promote fat loss and improve endurance by using fat as a primary fuel source.
- **Supplements:** Fighters often use dietary supplements like protein powders, branched-chain amino acids (BCAAs), and vitamins to support their training and recovery.

In the competitive world of the UFC, fighters are constantly seeking innovative training methods to gain an advantage over their opponents. Whether it's high-altitude training, unique strength and conditioning techniques, mental preparation, or specialized diets, these methods reflect the dedication and commitment of UFC athletes to achieve greatness inside the octagon.

Chapter 86: Fighter Safety and UFC's Dedicated Medical Staff

Ensuring fighter safety is paramount in the UFC. To guarantee that fighters are in the best possible condition before, during, and after their bouts, the organization maintains a dedicated medical staff that provides comprehensive care and oversight.

Pre-Fight Medical Examinations

Before stepping into the octagon, fighters undergo a series of rigorous medical examinations. These examinations serve multiple purposes:

- **Physical Health Assessment:** Fighters are thoroughly examined to ensure they are in optimal physical condition to compete. This assessment includes checking for injuries, illnesses, and any pre-existing medical conditions that may affect their performance or safety.
- **Weight Check:** Fighters must make weight to compete in their designated weight class. UFC officials ensure that fighters meet these requirements safely without severe dehydration or drastic weight cuts that could endanger their health.
- **Neurological Evaluations:** To assess fighters' neurological health, pre-fight evaluations may include neurological exams,

including testing reflexes and cognitive function.

Fight-Night Medical Team

The UFC assembles a highly trained medical team for each event, consisting of physicians, paramedics, and other medical professionals. This team is responsible for monitoring fighters' health and responding to any medical emergencies that may arise during the event.

In-Fight Medical Assistance

During bouts, the medical team remains vigilant, ready to intervene if a fighter sustains an injury or displays signs of distress. The "cutman" is another essential member of this team, responsible for treating fighters' cuts and wounds to prevent them from worsening.

Post-Fight Medical Evaluations

Fighters are subjected to post-fight medical evaluations immediately after their bouts. These evaluations are critical for detecting injuries that may have occurred during the fight, such as concussions, fractures, or soft tissue injuries.

Medical Suspensions

Based on the findings of post-fight medical evaluations, fighters may receive medical suspensions that prevent them from competing until they have fully recovered. These suspensions are essential to protect fighters from further harm and ensure they are fit to return to the octagon.

Strict Drug Testing Protocols

To maintain fighter safety and integrity, the UFC collaborates with the United States Anti-Doping Agency (USADA) to implement strict drug testing protocols. Fighters are subject to random drug tests, both in and out of competition, to detect the use of performance-enhancing substances or other prohibited drugs. This testing helps ensure a level playing field and safeguards fighters' health.

Fighter Education

The UFC also emphasizes fighter education on health and safety issues. Fighters receive guidance on weight management, nutrition, hydration, and injury prevention. This educational component contributes to safer training and competition practices.

Medical Innovations

The UFC continually explores medical innovations and technologies to enhance fighter safety. This includes advancements in equipment, medical procedures, and injury rehabilitation techniques.

In the UFC, fighter safety is not just a priority; it's a fundamental principle. The dedicated medical staff and comprehensive safety measures in place serve as a testament to the organization's commitment to protecting the well-being of its athletes.

Chapter 87: Championship Bouts as UFC Main Events

The Ultimate Fighting Championship (UFC) is renowned for its high-stakes championship bouts, which often serve as the main event of major fight cards. These title fights are the pinnacle of mixed martial arts (MMA) competition and capture the attention of fans worldwide. In this chapter, we delve into the significance of championship bouts in the UFC.

A Champion's Reward: The Main Event

Headlining the Card: Championship fights are typically featured as the main event of UFC events. They occupy the most prominent position on the fight card and are the focal point of the entire event.

Five-Round Thrillers: Unlike non-title fights, which consist of three rounds, championship bouts extend to five rounds. This format allows fighters to showcase their skills over a more extended period and often leads to epic battles.

Champion vs. Challenger: The championship fight features the reigning champion defending their title against a top-ranked challenger. This dynamic creates a unique blend of tension and excitement, as the champion strives to maintain their dominance while the challenger aims to dethrone them.

Variety of Weight Classes and Titles

Multiple Weight Classes: The UFC features multiple weight classes for both men and women, each with its own championship title. This diversity ensures that fans can enjoy championship bouts in various weight divisions, from the featherweight (145 pounds) to the heavyweight (over 205 pounds) categories.

Interim Titles: In cases where a champion is unable to defend their title due to injury or other reasons, the UFC may introduce an interim title. This allows top contenders to compete for a temporary championship, ensuring that the division remains active.

Historic Moments in Championship History

Iconic Title Fights: The UFC has witnessed numerous historic championship bouts that have left an indelible mark on the sport. These include battles like Anderson Silva vs. Chael Sonnen, Ronda Rousey vs. Holly Holm, and Jon Jones vs. Alexander Gustafsson.

Changing of the Guard: Championship fights often mark pivotal moments in a fighter's career. They can signify the ascent of a new champion or the continuation of a reigning champion's legacy.

Draw of the Titles: What's at Stake

Prestige and Recognition: Winning a UFC championship is the pinnacle of achievement in MMA.

It bestows prestige upon the victor and cements their place in the annals of combat sports history.

Financial Rewards: Championship fights often come with substantial financial incentives. Fighters earn more for title bouts, reflecting the high stakes and the pressure to perform at the highest level.

Fan Engagement and Excitement

Fan Favorites: Championship bouts consistently draw high viewership and attendance numbers. Fans are eager to witness the crowning of new champions or the successful defense of titles by their favorite fighters.

Emotional Investment: The narratives surrounding championship fights, including the champions' journeys and the challenges posed by challengers, evoke strong emotions among fans. These emotional connections contribute to the sport's enduring popularity.

Championship bouts in the UFC are more than just fights; they are the culmination of fighters' dreams, the embodiment of dedication and skill, and the source of unforgettable moments in combat sports history. As long as the UFC continues to showcase these high-stakes contests, fans can expect the excitement and drama of championship bouts to endure.

Chapter 88: The UFC's Merchandise Line

The Ultimate Fighting Championship (UFC) has established itself not only as a premier mixed martial arts (MMA) organization but also as a brand with a diverse range of merchandise. In this chapter, we explore the world of UFC merchandise, from clothing and accessories to collectibles.

UFC Apparel: Style Inside and Outside the Octagon

Fighter Walkout Apparel: One of the most popular categories of UFC merchandise is fighter walkout apparel. These are the shirts, shorts, and hoodies that fighters wear when entering the Octagon. Fans can purchase these items to show support for their favorite fighters.

Fan Apparel: The UFC offers a wide variety of clothing for fans, including t-shirts, hats, jackets, and more. These items feature the UFC logo, fighter names, and event-specific designs.

Performance Gear: In addition to casual apparel, the UFC has a line of performance gear designed for athletes and fitness enthusiasts. This includes compression wear, training shorts, and workout gear.

Accessories and Collectibles

Accessories: UFC merchandise extends beyond clothing. Fans can find a range of accessories, including bags, backpacks, water bottles, and phone cases, all branded with the UFC logo.

Collectibles: For dedicated fans and collectors, the UFC offers a range of collectible items. These may include autographed memorabilia, trading cards, action figures, and posters from iconic fights.

Customizable Gear

Personalized Apparel: Some UFC merchandise can be customized with the names and numbers of favorite fighters or even personal text, allowing fans to create unique, one-of-a-kind items.

International Reach

Global Availability: UFC merchandise is not limited to the United States. The organization has a global fan base, and its merchandise is available internationally, allowing fans from around the world to support their favorite fighters and the UFC brand.

Online and Event Sales

Official UFC Store: The primary source for UFC merchandise is the official UFC store, which operates online and at select events. This store provides fans with access to the latest and most extensive range of UFC merchandise.

Event Merchandise: When attending live UFC events, fans have the opportunity to purchase event-specific merchandise, including shirts and souvenirs related to that particular fight card.

Revenue and Brand Building

Financial Impact: The sale of UFC merchandise generates substantial revenue for the organization. This income contributes to the growth and development of the sport.

Brand Recognition: UFC merchandise serves as a branding tool, helping to spread awareness of the sport and the UFC brand. Fans wearing UFC gear become walking advertisements for the organization.

Fan Connection

Fan Engagement: UFC merchandise allows fans to connect more deeply with the sport and their favorite fighters. Wearing a fighter's shirt or using UFC accessories is a way for fans to express their passion.

Event Souvenirs: Attending a live UFC event and purchasing event-specific merchandise is a memorable experience for fans. These items serve as souvenirs of the event.

The UFC's merchandise line has become an integral part of the sport's culture, offering fans a tangible connection to their favorite fighters and the organization itself. Whether it's donning the walkout apparel of a beloved champion or collecting limited edition items, UFC merchandise provides fans with a unique way to celebrate their passion for MMA and the UFC.

Chapter 89: Fighters Turned Coaches

In the world of MMA and the UFC, fighters often find themselves at a crossroads when their active fighting careers come to an end. For many, the transition from fighter to coach is a natural and rewarding progression. In this chapter, we explore how some fighters transition into coaching roles after retiring from competition.

The Role of a Coach

Mentoring Future Generations: Fighters who become coaches take on a crucial role in shaping the next generation of MMA talent. They pass on their knowledge, skills, and experience to aspiring fighters.

Strategy and Game Planning: Coaches play a pivotal role in developing fight strategies and game plans for their fighters. They analyze opponents, identify weaknesses, and help fighters prepare mentally and physically.

Coaching at MMA Gyms

MMA Gyms: Many fighters transition into coaching roles at established MMA gyms. These gyms often serve as breeding grounds for talent and provide a structured environment for fighters to develop their coaching skills.

Technical Training: Fighter-coaches work on technical aspects such as striking, grappling, and conditioning with their students. They may specialize in specific disciplines like Brazilian Jiu-Jitsu, Muay Thai, or wrestling.

Notable Fighter-Coaches

Matt Serra: A former UFC Welterweight Champion, Matt Serra transitioned to coaching and is known for his work with fighters like Chris Weidman and Aljamain Sterling. His guidance has led to several championship victories.

Duane Ludwig: Duane "Bang" Ludwig, a skilled striker, became a renowned coach at Team Alpha Male. His focus on striking techniques has transformed many fighters into formidable stand-up competitors.

Training Camps

Fighter Camps: Some fighters who retire from active competition choose to run their own training camps. These camps attract fighters seeking personalized coaching and a tailored approach to their development.

Personalized Coaching: Training camps run by former fighters often emphasize individualized coaching, allowing fighters to work on weaknesses and refine their strengths.

Mentoring Beyond Technique

Mentorship and Personal Growth: Fighter-coaches often serve as mentors beyond the gym, helping fighters navigate the mental and emotional challenges of the sport. They offer guidance on discipline, work ethic, and resilience.

Transition Challenges

Adjusting to Coaching: Transitioning from being an athlete to a coach can be challenging. Fighters must adapt to a different role that requires them to guide, instruct, and motivate others.

Balancing Coaching and Personal Life: Coaching demands time and dedication. Fighter-coaches often face the challenge of balancing coaching responsibilities with their personal lives.

Legacy and Impact

Building a Coaching Legacy: A fighter's impact as a coach can be just as significant as their impact in the Octagon. They leave behind a legacy through the achievements of their students.

Contributions to the Sport: Fighter-coaches contribute to the growth and evolution of MMA. Their expertise and teaching shape the sport and its future.

The transition from fighter to coach is a testament to the enduring passion and commitment of those who have dedicated their lives to MMA. As these fighter-coaches pass on their knowledge and experiences to the next generation of fighters, they continue to play a vital role in the ever-evolving world of mixed martial arts.

Chapter 90: Fighter Safety First - The UFC's Dedicated Medical Staff

In the fast-paced, hard-hitting world of mixed martial arts and the Ultimate Fighting Championship, fighter safety is paramount. To ensure the well-being of athletes who step into the Octagon, the UFC has established a dedicated medical staff and rigorous safety protocols. In this chapter, we delve into the critical role played by the UFC's medical professionals in safeguarding fighter health.

The UFC's Commitment to Fighter Safety

Pre-fight Medical Evaluations: Before fighters even step into the Octagon, they undergo thorough medical evaluations. These assessments include physical examinations, neurological tests, and comprehensive medical histories.

Weight Cutting Oversight: The UFC's medical staff closely monitors the weight-cutting process to prevent extreme dehydration and dangerous practices. Fighters are required to meet specific hydration levels.

Medical Professionals Ringside

Ringside Physicians: UFC events feature licensed ringside physicians who are experts in combat sports medicine. They are stationed cageside and are ready to provide immediate medical attention if needed.

Emergency Medical Teams: In case of severe injuries or medical emergencies, the UFC has emergency medical teams on standby. These teams are equipped to handle a wide range of critical situations.

Fighter Recovery

Post-fight Medical Examinations: After a fight, fighters receive post-fight medical examinations to assess any injuries or health concerns. This is done to ensure that fighters are fit to compete again.

Medical Suspensions: If a fighter sustains injuries during a bout, the UFC's medical staff may impose medical suspensions. These suspensions vary in duration based on the severity of the injury and are intended to allow fighters ample time to recover.

Fighter Welfare

Mental Health Support: Fighter safety extends beyond physical health. The UFC recognizes the importance of mental well-being and provides access to mental health professionals for fighters who may need support.

Health and Nutrition Guidance: The UFC's medical staff offers guidance on healthy weight management, nutrition, and injury prevention to help fighters maintain their well-being.

Research and Innovation

Continuous Research: The UFC invests in research to enhance fighter safety. This includes studies on head trauma, injury prevention, and weight-cutting practices to inform policies and protocols.

Innovative Safety Gear: The UFC explores cutting-edge safety gear and technologies to further protect fighters during competition.

Educational Initiatives

Fighter Education: The UFC provides educational programs to fighters on topics like concussion awareness, anti-doping, and general health and safety.

Referee and Official Training: The UFC's medical staff also trains referees and officials to recognize signs of injury or distress during a fight, ensuring prompt medical attention.

Collaboration with Athletic Commissions

Working with Athletic Commissions: The UFC collaborates closely with state athletic commissions to adhere to and often exceed regulatory requirements, ensuring the highest standards of safety.

Medical Data Sharing: The UFC shares anonymized medical data and research findings with commissions to contribute to broader fighter safety initiatives in combat sports.

The UFC's commitment to fighter safety goes beyond the confines of the Octagon. With a dedicated medical staff, stringent protocols, and a focus on research and education, the organization strives to set industry standards and prioritize the health and well-being of its athletes.

Chapter 91: Championship Bouts - The Epic Main Events of UFC Events

In the world of mixed MMA and the UFC, championship bouts are the pinnacle of competition. These high-stakes encounters serve as the main events of UFC events, drawing fans from around the globe who eagerly anticipate the crowning of a new champion or the defense of an existing title. In this chapter, we'll explore the significance of championship bouts in the UFC, examining their history, impact, and what makes them an integral part of MMA's appeal.

The Prestige of Championship Bouts

Crowning Champions: Championship bouts determine the best fighters in their respective weight classes. Victory in these fights signifies excellence and dominance in the division.

Fan Excitement: Championship bouts generate intense excitement and anticipation among fans. They often serve as the primary motivation for fans to purchase tickets, tune in on TV, or attend live events.

The Types of UFC Championships

Weight Classes: UFC championships are awarded across various weight classes, ranging from the featherweight division to the heavyweight division. Each weight class has its own champion.

Men and Women: The UFC introduced women's divisions in 2013, extending the prestige of championship bouts to female fighters as well.

Historical Significance

UFC 12 - Birth of Titles: The UFC introduced its first titles at UFC 12 in 1997. Mark Coleman became the first UFC Heavyweight Champion, and Maurice Smith claimed the UFC Heavyweight Championship.

Legendary Champions: The annals of UFC history are filled with legendary champions like Anderson Silva, Georges St-Pierre, Ronda Rousey, and Jon Jones, who have cemented their legacies with numerous title defenses.

The Main Event Spotlight

Headlining the Card: Championship bouts typically serve as the main event, concluding the evening's festivities with a bang. They are strategically placed to maximize viewership.

Five-Round Fights: To ensure a fair and definitive result, championship bouts are scheduled for five rounds, as opposed to the standard three rounds for non-title fights.

Title Changes and Defenses

Iconic Upsets: Championship bouts have witnessed some of the most memorable upsets in UFC history.

These shocking victories, where underdogs dethrone champions, captivate fans worldwide.

Title Defenses: Champion fighters face the daunting task of defending their titles against hungry contenders. Successful title defenses solidify their positions as dominant figures in the sport.

Fighter Legacies

Legacy-Building: Winning a championship and defending it multiple times cements a fighter's legacy as one of the all-time greats.

Title Reigns: Some champions enjoy historic title reigns, like Anderson Silva's 2,457-day stint as the UFC Middleweight Champion.

Championship Bouts as Milestones

Milestones in UFC History: Iconic championship bouts mark significant milestones in the UFC's journey from a fringe sport to global recognition.

Global Appeal: UFC championship bouts have a global appeal, transcending borders and cultures, with fans from all corners of the world tuning in.

Championship Bouts and Pay-Per-View Sales

PPV Attraction: Championship bouts are major attractions for pay-per-view (PPV) sales. These high-profile fights contribute significantly to the financial success of UFC events.

Record-Setting Bouts: Some championship bouts have set records for PPV buys, showcasing their drawing power.

The Drama of the Walkout

Fighter Walkouts: Championship bouts often feature dramatic walkouts with special music, lighting, and fanfare, adding to the spectacle.

Champion's Walkout: The reigning champion's walkout is a moment of pride, signaling their readiness to defend their title.

Championship bouts are the beating heart of the UFC, captivating fans with their intensity, drama, and historic significance. They showcase the pinnacle of combat sports and elevate fighters to legendary status, leaving an indelible mark on the world of MMA.

Chapter 92: The Thriving World of UFC Merchandise

In the world of combat sports, few organizations can rival the UFC's ability to create a global brand. Beyond the octagon battles and the roar of the crowd, the UFC has extended its presence to a wide array of merchandise that fans can proudly wear and display. In this chapter, we'll delve into the thriving world of UFC merchandise.

UFC's Merchandising Powerhouse

The UFC, with its immense fan base and worldwide reach, has become a merchandising powerhouse. From clothing and accessories to collectibles and even branded training gear, there's a wide range of UFC merchandise available to cater to fans of all ages and tastes.

Iconic Logo and Slogans

At the heart of UFC merchandise is its iconic logo, featuring a bold, stylized silhouette of a fighter within an octagon. This logo has become synonymous with the sport and is instantly recognizable to fans around the world. Additionally, the UFC has coined several slogans and catchphrases that often find their way onto merchandise, further cementing the brand's identity.

Fighter Apparel

One of the most popular categories of UFC merchandise is fighter apparel. Fans can purchase clothing and accessories featuring their favorite fighters' names and images. This includes everything from T-shirts and hoodies to hats and gloves. Wearing a fighter's gear is a way for fans to show their support and connect with their idols.

Event-Specific Merchandise

The UFC produces event-specific merchandise for many of its major cards. These items are often limited-edition and commemorate specific fights or events. Fans who attend live events can purchase these exclusive collectibles as lasting mementos of their UFC experience.

Collectibles and Memorabilia

For dedicated fans and collectors, UFC merchandise goes beyond clothing. Collectibles and memorabilia are highly sought after. This category includes autographed fight posters, trading cards, and even replica championship belts. Owning a piece of UFC history is a dream come true for many enthusiasts.

UFC Gyms and Training Gear

The UFC has expanded its brand into the fitness world with the creation of UFC Gyms. These gyms offer specialized training programs and equipment, and they also sell branded training gear and apparel. Fans can work out in style with equipment bearing the UFC logo.

Online and In-Person Availability

UFC merchandise is readily available both online and at live events. The official UFC website offers a vast selection of items for purchase, and many sporting goods stores also carry UFC gear. Live events, including Fight Nights and pay-per-view cards, often have merchandise booths where fans can shop in person.

Global Appeal

What sets UFC merchandise apart is its global appeal. The UFC's fan base spans continents, and merchandise is designed with this diversity in mind. Fans from different cultures and backgrounds can find items that resonate with them, making the UFC's brand truly international.

Community and Camaraderie

Wearing UFC merchandise is more than just fashion; it's a way for fans to feel a part of the UFC community. Whether watching fights at home or attending live events, fans proudly display their UFC gear, creating a sense of camaraderie among enthusiasts worldwide.

The Future of UFC Merchandise

As the UFC continues to grow and evolve, so too will its merchandise offerings. New fighters will rise to stardom, legendary battles will be fought, and the brand will expand into new markets. Through it all,

UFC merchandise will remain an integral part of the sport, allowing fans to connect with the excitement and energy of mixed martial arts.

In this chapter, we've explored the diverse world of UFC merchandise, from fighter apparel to collectibles and beyond. As fans continue to support their favorite fighters and the sport itself, UFC merchandise will play a central role in celebrating the passion and dedication of the UFC community.

Chapter 93: Celebrity Ownership in the UFC

While the UFC is primarily known for its fighters and combat sports, it has also caught the attention of several celebrities who have chosen to invest in the organization. These celebrities have not only added a touch of glamour but also brought their business acumen into the world of mixed martial arts (MMA). In this chapter, we'll delve into the realm of celebrity ownership within the UFC and explore some of the notable names associated with the organization.

Celebrity Investors: A Surprising Mix

Ben Affleck: The Oscar-winning actor, director, and screenwriter, Ben Affleck, has publicly expressed his interest in the UFC. His involvement demonstrates the diverse range of celebrity owners within the organization.

Tom Brady: Widely regarded as one of the greatest quarterbacks in NFL history, Tom Brady has ventured into the world of MMA by investing in the UFC. His strategic mind in football appears to extend to the business arena.

Calvin Harris: The world-renowned DJ and music producer, Calvin Harris, has made a name for himself in the electronic dance music scene. His involvement in the UFC highlights the global reach and appeal of the organization.

Jimmy Kimmel: The late-night talk show host and comedian, Jimmy Kimmel, is known for his humorous take on various topics. His investment in the UFC showcases the broad spectrum of celebrities interested in the sport.

Unexpected Connections

Maria Sharapova: The former world No. 1 professional tennis player, Maria Sharapova, may not be an obvious choice for a UFC investor, but her participation illustrates the diverse interests of celebrities and their willingness to diversify their portfolios.

Venus and Serena Williams: The tennis superstar sisters, Venus and Serena Williams, have made significant contributions to their sport. Their involvement in the UFC ownership group demonstrates their entrepreneurial spirit.

The Business of MMA

Investment Strategy: Celebrity ownership in the UFC is not just a matter of prestige but also a strategic business move. The organization's global reach and potential for growth make it an attractive investment opportunity.

Promotion and Marketing: Celebrities associated with the UFC often play a role in promoting the sport, attending events, and endorsing fighters. Their star power can help expand the UFC's fan base.

A Sense of Belonging

Shared Passion: Many of these celebrity investors share a genuine passion for MMA and the UFC. Their involvement goes beyond financial interests and reflects a deeper connection to the sport.

Building a Legacy: UFC ownership provides celebrities with an opportunity to be part of the legacy of a sport that has grown from its humble beginnings into a global phenomenon.

The Future of Celebrity Ownership

Continued Growth: As the UFC continues to expand its global footprint and reach new heights in the world of combat sports, it's likely that more celebrities will express interest in becoming part of the organization.

Diverse Perspectives: Celebrity ownership brings diverse perspectives and experiences into the UFC's inner circle, enriching its leadership with fresh ideas and insights.

The presence of celebrities as UFC investors not only underscores the organization's appeal but also adds a layer of intrigue to the world of MMA. Their involvement serves as a testament to the global reach and business potential of the UFC, reinforcing its status as a premier organization in the world of combat sports.

Chapter 94: UFC Fighter Safety and the Absence of Fatalities

The UFC is undoubtedly a brutal sport, but it's also one where the safety of its athletes is paramount. One remarkable fact about the UFC is that, despite the intense nature of mixed martial arts (MMA) competition, no UFC fighter has ever died in the octagon. This remarkable safety record is the result of rigorous safety measures and protocols in place.

Medical Staff and Pre-Fight Examinations

Before each fight, fighters undergo extensive medical examinations. These exams include detailed physicals, neurological tests, and eye exams to ensure fighters are physically fit to compete. A team of experienced doctors and medical staff is present at every event, ready to provide immediate attention if needed.

Weight Cutting Regulations

Weight cutting, a common practice among fighters to meet their designated weight class, can pose health risks. To mitigate this, the UFC has implemented strict weight-cutting regulations. These regulations include early weigh-ins, multiple weigh-in checks, and penalties for fighters who miss weight. This helps ensure fighters enter the octagon in a healthier state.

Concussion Protocols

In recent years, the UFC has also implemented rigorous concussion protocols. Fighters suspected of suffering a concussion are subject to thorough evaluation, and they must be cleared by a medical professional before returning to competition. This is a critical step in protecting fighters from the long-term effects of head trauma.

Fighter Safety Beyond the Octagon

Fighter safety extends beyond the confines of the octagon. The UFC provides medical insurance for fighters, covering any injuries sustained during their fights and, in some cases, even beyond. This comprehensive coverage helps fighters recover and rehabilitate without the burden of medical expenses.

Continual Improvement

The UFC remains committed to fighter safety and continually looks for ways to improve its safety measures. This includes working with organizations like the Professional Fighters Brain Health Study to better understand the long-term effects of combat sports and implement further safety measures.

Chapter 95: Becoming a UFC Gym Owner

If you're a fan of mixed martial arts and dream of owning a piece of the action, you might be surprised to learn that you can become the owner of a UFC Gym. This chapter will provide detailed information on how this dream can become a reality, outlining the initial costs, the investment required, and what it takes to own a part of one of the fastest-growing sports franchises in the world.

The UFC Gym Franchise Opportunity

The UFC Gym is part of the larger UFC brand, which has experienced explosive growth in the world of combat sports. UFC Gyms offer a unique fitness experience, combining traditional gym offerings with mixed martial arts training and classes. This combination has attracted a diverse and dedicated membership base.

Initial Costs

Becoming a UFC Gym owner starts with understanding the initial costs involved. While owning a piece of the UFC Gym brand can be lucrative, it's not without its financial requirements. The initial franchise fee typically ranges from $30,000 to $50,000, depending on various factors such as location and size.

Investment Range

In addition to the franchise fee, potential owners should be prepared for an estimated total investment ranging from $100,000 to $2 million. This investment covers everything from equipment and facility build-out to marketing and operational expenses. The wide range in investment reflects the flexibility of the UFC Gym franchise model, which can cater to both smaller, single-location facilities and larger, more comprehensive fitness centers.

Location, Location, Location

One of the key factors in the success of a UFC Gym franchise is its location. UFC Gyms are typically found in areas with high foot traffic, a diverse population, and a strong interest in fitness and martial arts. Choosing the right location is crucial to attracting members and ensuring the success of your investment.

Training and Support

Becoming a UFC Gym owner isn't just about the financial investment; it also requires dedication and a passion for the brand. UFC provides training and support to franchisees, helping them navigate the complexities of owning and operating a gym. From marketing and branding to hiring and training staff, UFC offers guidance every step of the way.

The UFC Gym Experience

UFC Gyms provide a unique fitness experience for members. They offer a variety of classes and training programs, including mixed martial arts, Brazilian Jiu-Jitsu, boxing, kickboxing, and general fitness classes. The gyms are known for their state-of-the-art equipment and facilities, making them appealing to fitness enthusiasts of all levels.

Success Stories

Throughout the years, several UFC Gym franchisees have found success and satisfaction in owning their piece of the UFC brand. These success stories often involve passionate individuals who combined their love for fitness and martial arts with a strong entrepreneurial spirit.

Becoming a UFC Gym owner can be an exciting and rewarding venture for those with the financial means and dedication to make it happen. With the right location, investment, and commitment to the UFC brand, you can be a part of the ever-growing world of mixed martial arts and fitness.

If you're considering this path, it's essential to do thorough research, seek guidance from UFC representatives, and carefully assess your financial capabilities. With the right approach, you could soon be the proud owner of a UFC Gym, contributing to the growth of this dynamic fitness and martial arts community.

Chapter 96: Record-Breaking Attendance at UFC 243

In the world of mixed martial arts, the UFC is known for hosting monumental events that capture the imagination of fans worldwide. One such historic event that etched its name in the annals of UFC history is UFC 243, which took place in Melbourne, Australia, in 2019. This chapter explores how UFC 243 became the highest-attended event in UFC history up to that point, leaving an indelible mark on the sport.

Setting the Stage: Marvel Stadium, Melbourne

The stage for this record-breaking event was Marvel Stadium, an iconic sports and entertainment venue located in Melbourne. This massive stadium, with a seating capacity that can accommodate over 53,000 spectators, is renowned for hosting a variety of sporting events, including cricket, Australian rules football, and concerts.

UFC 243: Whittaker vs. Adesanya

UFC 243 was headlined by a highly anticipated matchup between two elite fighters: Robert Whittaker and Israel Adesanya. Whittaker, the reigning UFC Middleweight Champion at the time, was defending his title against the surging challenger, Adesanya. This championship clash generated immense excitement and anticipation within the MMA community and beyond.

A Landmark Moment: The Attendance Record

UFC 243 made history by shattering the previous attendance record for a UFC event. With a staggering 57,127 fans in attendance, it became the highest-attended event in UFC history at that time. The electric atmosphere within Marvel Stadium was palpable as fans from all corners of the globe converged to witness this extraordinary night of fights.

The International Appeal

The record attendance at UFC 243 highlighted the international appeal of the sport and the UFC brand. Fans from Australia and New Zealand, in particular, showed unwavering support for their fighters, contributing significantly to the event's success. The presence of local hero Robert Whittaker added to the fervor, as Australian fans rallied behind their champion.

The Fight Card: Memorable Moments

Aside from the epic main event, UFC 243 featured a compelling fight card filled with memorable moments. Knockouts, submissions, and back-and-forth battles captivated the audience throughout the evening. These fights showcased the depth and talent within the UFC roster, further solidifying the promotion's status as the premier organization in MMA.

Adesanya's Victory and the Legacy of UFC 243

In the main event, Israel Adesanya emerged victorious, defeating Robert Whittaker by knockout. Adesanya's win not only earned him the UFC Middleweight Championship but also cemented his status as one of the sport's brightest stars. UFC 243 will forever be remembered as a pivotal moment in Adesanya's career and in the history of the UFC.

Impact and Legacy

UFC 243's record-breaking attendance remains a testament to the global appeal of mixed martial arts and the UFC's ability to draw fans from around the world. This event showcased the passion and dedication of MMA enthusiasts and further solidified the UFC's position as a dominant force in combat sports.

In conclusion, UFC 243 at Marvel Stadium in Melbourne, Australia, stands as a historic milestone in the UFC's journey. The record-breaking attendance and the memorable fights that unfolded that night continue to be celebrated by fight fans and serve as a reminder of the incredible moments the UFC has provided over the years.

Chapter 97: Dana White's Continued Ownership of UFC Shares

Mixed martial arts underwent a seismic shift in 2016 when the UFC was sold for a staggering $4 billion dollars. This historic sale marked a new era for the organization, but one key figure remained closely tied to the UFC even after the sale: Dana White. In this chapter, we delve into Dana White's ownership of UFC shares and how he continues to play a pivotal role in the sport.

The Sale of UFC: A Monumental Deal

In July 2016, the UFC changed hands in what was one of the most significant acquisitions in sports history. The Fertitta brothers, Lorenzo and Frank, who had owned the majority of the organization's shares, decided to sell their stake. The buyers were the talent agency WME-IMG (now Endeavor), along with other investors.

Dana White's Role as UFC President

Throughout its meteoric rise, Dana White had been the public face and driving force behind the UFC. As the promotion's president, White played an instrumental role in its growth and popularity. His charismatic leadership and unwavering commitment to the sport endeared him to fighters and fans alike.

Dana White's Share Sale

With the sale of the UFC, it was widely reported that Dana White also sold a significant portion of his shares in the organization. The exact amount and financial details of his share sale were not publicly disclosed, but it was a lucrative transaction for the UFC president.

Dana White's Continued Ownership

While Dana White sold a substantial portion of his UFC shares, he did not divest himself entirely from the organization he had helped build. Instead, he retained ownership of a certain number of shares. This decision highlighted his enduring commitment to the sport and his desire to remain connected to the UFC's future.

Remaining at the Helm

Dana White's ongoing ownership stake in the UFC has not only kept him financially invested in the promotion but also allowed him to continue steering the ship as its president. His leadership has been instrumental in the UFC's expansion into new markets, the signing of top-tier talent, and the growth of the sport on a global scale.

Dana White's Influence

As an owner and president, Dana White's influence within the UFC remains substantial. He continues to negotiate fighter contracts, promote events, and make critical decisions that shape the organization's direction. His passion for MMA and his dedication to elevating the sport have solidified his place as a central figure in the world of combat sports.

The Legacy of Dana White

Dana White's decision to retain ownership of UFC shares after the historic sale underscores his deep connection to the sport and his vision for its future. While the UFC has evolved and expanded, White's unwavering dedication to MMA and his ongoing ownership stake serve as a testament to his enduring impact on the sport.

In the ever-evolving world of mixed martial arts, Dana White's dual role as an owner and president continues to be a defining feature of the UFC's identity. His journey from a struggling MMA enthusiast to a key figure in a multi-billion-dollar sports empire remains a remarkable story within the sport's history.

Chapter 98: UFC Fight Night 55 and UFC 224 - Record-Setting Finishes

Mixed martial arts is a sport renowned for its thrilling finishes and action-packed bouts. Among the countless events that have graced the UFC's history, two stand out for their exceptional number of finishes: UFC Fight Night 55 and UFC 224. In this chapter, we explore these two landmark events and the record-breaking finishes they delivered.

UFC Fight Night 55: The Perfect Finish Rate

UFC Fight Night 55, held on November 8, 2014, in Sydney, Australia, will forever be etched in MMA history for its remarkable achievement. This event boasted a perfect finish rate, with all 11 fights on the card concluding via stoppage. This astounding feat captured the imagination of fight fans worldwide.

The Night of Submissions and Knockouts

UFC Fight Night 55 featured an array of finishes, showcasing the diverse skills of the fighters. Submissions, the art of forcing an opponent to tap out, were a prominent theme. Fighters like Luke Rockhold, Al Iaquinta, and Jake Matthews secured submission victories that night, adding to the event's mystique.

Knockouts, the most electrifying form of finish, were also in abundance. Fighters such as Robert Whittaker and Clint Hester displayed their striking prowess, thrilling the audience with their stunning knockout victories. The combination of submissions and knockouts created an unforgettable night of action.

UFC 224: Another Spectacular Finish Fest

Moving forward to UFC 224, held on May 12, 2018, in Rio de Janeiro, Brazil, fight fans were treated to yet another incredible display of finishing ability. This event witnessed an astounding 13 finishes out of 13 fights, setting a record for the highest finish rate in UFC history.

A Night of Exceptional Performances

UFC 224 showcased the exceptional talent within the promotion. Fighters like Amanda Nunes, Lyoto Machida, and John Lineker delivered memorable performances. Nunes successfully defended her bantamweight title with a knockout victory, solidifying her status as one of the sport's top fighters.

In addition to Nunes's victory, the night featured a mix of submissions and knockouts that left fans in awe. The fighters on the card displayed their skill and determination, resulting in a finish rate that may never be equaled.

Legacy of Excitement

UFC Fight Night 55 and UFC 224 remain iconic events in UFC history, primarily because of their exceptional finish rates. These events showcased the essence of

MMA, where anything can happen inside the Octagon. They serve as a reminder of the excitement and unpredictability that fans cherish in the sport.

As MMA continues to evolve, fans eagerly anticipate future events that may challenge these records. Whether it's via submissions, knockouts, or a combination of both, one thing is certain: the thrill of the finish is a fundamental aspect of what makes the UFC the premier organization in mixed martial arts.

Chapter 99: UFC and the Unexplored Weight Classes

When it comes to the world of mixed martial arts (MMA), the Ultimate Fighting Championship (UFC) reigns supreme, earning its place as the most prominent and influential organization in the sport. However, there's an aspect where the UFC doesn't dictate the rules, and that's the weight classes. Contrary to what some might think, the UFC doesn't have the final say in determining the weight classes; it adheres to the regulations established by various athletic commissions.

Unified Rules of MMA and the Weight Classes

The Unified Rules of MMA serve as the standard guidelines governing the sport. These rules are formulated and maintained by an array of athletic commissions and organizations, not the UFC alone. Within these rules, there are a total of 13 recognized weight classes. These weight classes cater to fighters of all sizes and have been meticulously designed to ensure fair and competitive matchups.

UFC's Incomplete Weight Class Roster

While the UFC is undoubtedly the global MMA leader, it doesn't encompass all the weight classes recognized by the Unified Rules of MMA. Currently, the UFC includes eight weight classes for men and four for women. However, it's intriguing to note that among the men's weight classes, five remain unrepresented within the organization.

Here are the missing weight classes that the UFC could potentially include in the future:

Cruiserweight (225 lbs): A weight class between light heavyweight and heavyweight, catering to fighters who fall within the 205 to 225 lbs range.

Super Middleweight (195 lbs): A class designed for fighters between middleweight and light heavyweight, with an upper weight limit of 195 lbs.

Super Lightweight (165 lbs): An intermediary class straddling the lightweight and welterweight divisions, with a cap at 165 lbs.

Strawweight (115 lbs): The women's strawweight division is already part of the UFC, but it's important to recognize its inclusion in the Unified Rules of MMA, highlighting the UFC's alignment with these regulations.

Super Heavyweight (N/A): This is a unique weight class with no upper limit, allowing fighters who surpass the heavyweight threshold to compete without restrictions.

The UFC's Flexibility

The UFC's ability to incorporate weight classes as seen fit is a testament to its flexibility and its commitment to adapting to the evolving landscape of MMA. While it doesn't currently include all recognized weight classes, this could change in the future. The addition of new divisions is always a topic of discussion among MMA enthusiasts, and the UFC remains open to adjusting its roster as the sport continues to grow.

The UFC, despite its preeminence in the world of MMA, adheres to the weight class regulations outlined by various athletic commissions. While the organization doesn't currently feature all recognized weight classes, it possesses the flexibility to adapt and potentially expand its roster in the future, enhancing the depth and diversity of the fighters within its ranks.

Chapter 100: UFC's Strategic Investment in China

China, with its vast population and deep-rooted martial arts traditions, presents an enticing opportunity for the UFC. The organization recognized the untapped potential of this market and embarked on a journey to establish a firm foothold. Several key initiatives have contributed to the UFC's expanding influence in China:

Recruitment of Chinese Fighters

The UFC has actively scouted and signed Chinese fighters, introducing them to the global stage. This not only provides Chinese fighters with a platform to showcase their skills but also piques the interest of local fans.

Collaborations and Partnerships

To navigate the intricacies of the Chinese market, the UFC has formed partnerships and collaborations with local organizations and sports entities. These alliances facilitate the promotion of UFC events and talent in the region.

UFC Performance Institute Shanghai

The UFC's commitment to athlete development is evident in its establishment of the UFC Performance Institute in Shanghai. This state-of-the-art facility offers training and support services to both Chinese and international fighters.

Chinese Fighters Making an Impact

One of the clearest indicators of the UFC's success in China is the rising prominence of Chinese fighters on the global stage. These athletes have not only joined the UFC but have also achieved notable success, capturing the attention of fans worldwide. Some of the prominent Chinese fighters in the UFC include:

Weili Zhang

Zhang made history by becoming the first Chinese UFC champion. She secured the strawweight title, further solidifying her nation's presence in the MMA world.

Li Jingliang

Known for his exciting fighting style, Li Jingliang has been a consistent performer in the UFC's welterweight division.

Song Yadong

This young prospect has showcased his skills and potential, earning recognition as a fighter to watch in the UFC's bantamweight division.

The UFC's Ongoing Commitment

The UFC's investments in China are not limited to short-term gains. The organization envisions a long and prosperous relationship with the Chinese market. This commitment extends beyond signing fighters; it involves cultivating a fan base, organizing events, and nurturing the growth of MMA as a mainstream sport in China.

The UFC's strategic investment in China reflects its recognition of the immense potential within this market. Through recruitment efforts, collaborations, and the success of Chinese fighters, the UFC is steadily expanding its presence in China and contributing to the global growth of mixed martial arts. This commitment is a testament to the UFC's dedication to nurturing the sport's development on a global scale.

Chapter 101: The UFC's Legal Battles

While the UFC garners attention for its thrilling fights and superstar fighters, a less-publicized battle has been unfolding in the background. Many MMA fans are unaware that the UFC has been entangled in a series of lawsuits that could significantly impact the sport's future.

The Antitrust Lawsuit of 2014

The legal saga began in 2014 when former UFC fighter Cung Le and several others filed an antitrust lawsuit against Zuffa, the parent company of the UFC. Their primary contention was that the UFC operated as an illegal monopoly, systematically crushing competing MMA promoters globally. They alleged that this monopoly allowed the UFC to exert control over fighter wages, ultimately depressing their earnings.

The Class-Action Lawsuit

The antitrust lawsuit soon escalated into a class-action lawsuit, with additional fighters joining the legal battle. The plaintiffs argued that the UFC employed predatory practices that stifled competition and restricted fighters' earning potential. This case attracted considerable attention within the MMA community, as it had the potential to reshape the entire industry.

Settlement in 2018

After several years of legal wrangling and courtroom battles, the UFC reached a settlement in 2018, resolving the class-action lawsuit. While the terms of the settlement remain confidential, it marked a significant development in the ongoing legal struggles surrounding the organization.

Additional Lawsuits

Apart from the antitrust lawsuit, the UFC has faced legal challenges on other fronts as well. Some fighters have taken legal action against the promotion regarding issues like contract disputes and alleged anti-competitive behavior. These lawsuits underscore the complexities of fighter-promoter relationships in the world of MMA.

The Implications

The legal battles that the UFC has faced, particularly the antitrust lawsuit, have raised questions about the organization's business practices and their impact on fighters' livelihoods. While the settlement in 2018 resolved one major case, the UFC remains under scrutiny, and future legal challenges could shape the sport's landscape.

The Ongoing Struggle

Despite the settlement, the UFC continues to grapple with legal challenges. The issues surrounding fighter compensation, contract negotiations, and allegations of anti-competitive behavior persist. As the sport of MMA evolves, so too will the legal complexities that accompany it. The outcome of these lawsuits could influence the future direction of the UFC and the sport as a whole.

The legal battles facing the UFC serve as a reminder that behind the glitz and glamour of fight nights, there is a complex web of legal issues that can impact the fighters, the organization, and the sport itself. While the verdicts and settlements provide some resolution, the UFC's ongoing legal journey remains an integral part of its narrative.

Chapter 102: The Golden Legacy of UFC Belts

The UFC Championship belt is more than just a prize; it's a symbol of excellence, hard work, and dedication. The belts, coveted by fighters across the globe, hold a unique place in the world of combat sports. But what makes these belts so special? Is it true that they are made of real gold? In this chapter, we delve into the shimmering world of UFC belts.

The Prestigious Design

UFC Championship belts are renowned for their striking design and craftsmanship. These belts are much more than mere trinkets; they are works of art. Crafted to perfection, they embody the essence of MMA and the pinnacle of achievement within the sport.

The Gold Standard

The UFC Championship belts indeed contain real gold. While not entirely made of gold, they feature gold plating and are adorned with various gemstones. The belts represent the highest honor a fighter can achieve in the octagon, and the use of gold underscores their significance.

The Evolution of UFC Belts

Over the years, the design of UFC Championship belts has evolved. Each weight class has its unique belt design, with different gemstones and colors representing the various divisions. The changes in belt design reflect the UFC's commitment to innovation and the evolution of the sport.

A Legacy of Champions

Every fighter dreams of strapping a UFC Championship belt around their waist. These belts represent the culmination of years of hard work, dedication, and sacrifice. They are a testament to a fighter's journey and serve as a visual reminder of their place in the annals of MMA history.

The Magnetism of Gold

The inclusion of real gold in the UFC belts adds to their allure. Gold has long been associated with achievement, success, and victory. When a fighter is awarded a UFC Championship belt, they are not just receiving a trophy; they are taking possession of a piece of combat sports history, crafted from one of the world's most prized materials.

Beyond the Octagon

UFC Championship belts are not just symbols of victory; they are also valuable commodities. Some fighters, after winning a belt, have sold them for significant sums of money, while others proudly display them in their homes or gyms as a constant source of motivation.

A Legacy in Gold

The UFC Championship belts, with their real gold plating, are more than just rewards for fighters. They are symbols of excellence, dedication, and the enduring pursuit of greatness. These belts will continue to shine brightly in the world of MMA, serving as a reminder of the fighters who have etched their names in history and those who aspire to do so in the future.

In the world of UFC, gold is more than just a precious metal; it's a testament to the blood, sweat, and tears shed inside the octagon, and a symbol of the fighters' unwavering commitment to achieving greatness.

Chapter 103: The Sound of UFC: "Face the Pain" by Stemm

When you hear the ominous guitar riffs and intense drumbeats kick in, you know something significant is about to happen. For UFC fans, this is the moment they've been waiting for—the entrance of fighters into the octagon, and it's all accompanied by the iconic theme song, "Face the Pain" by Stemm. In this chapter, we delve into the story behind this unforgettable anthem.

The Birth of an Anthem

"Face the Pain" was introduced as the official UFC pay-per-view theme song in 2002. Its raw energy, aggressive vocals, and hard-hitting instrumentals perfectly captured the spirit of the sport and the intense emotions that accompany each fight.

Stemm: The Band Behind the Sound

Stemm, a heavy metal band hailing from Buffalo, New York, is the creative force behind "Face the Pain." The band consists of lead vocalist Joe Cafarella, guitarist Alex Scouten, bassist Kris Norris, and drummer Dan Nelligan. Their music, characterized by its heavy and aggressive sound, was a perfect fit for the UFC's no-holds-barred brand of combat.

Why "Face the Pain"?

The selection of "Face the Pain" as the UFC's theme song was not accidental. The song's aggressive tone and lyrics embody the intense physical and mental challenges fighters face when stepping into the octagon. It sets the stage for the battles that will unfold and serves as a psychological trigger for both fighters and fans.

Impact on the UFC Experience

"Face the Pain" has become an integral part of the UFC experience. It plays a crucial role in building anticipation and excitement as fighters make their way to the cage. The song has become synonymous with the sport, evoking a sense of adrenaline and anticipation among viewers.

Controversy and Fan Reception

While "Face the Pain" has its dedicated fan base within the UFC community, it has also faced its share of controversy. Some viewers have found the song's aggressive nature off-putting, while others believe it enhances the overall experience. Regardless of opinions, there's no denying its lasting impact.

The Evolution of UFC Themes

Over the years, the UFC has introduced various theme songs and soundtracks for its events. While "Face the Pain" remains an iconic anthem, the organization has occasionally experimented with different tracks to cater to changing tastes and to reflect the evolving nature of the sport.

Legacy in the Octagon

"Face the Pain" by Stemm is more than just a song; it's a battle cry, a prelude to combat, and an integral part of the UFC's identity. It continues to resonate with fans and fighters alike, encapsulating the essence of what it means to step into the octagon and face the pain.

The Power of Music

In the world of combat sports, music has the incredible power to set the stage, build anticipation, and evoke emotions. "Face the Pain" has mastered this art, leaving an indelible mark on the UFC and ensuring that, with every play, fans are ready to face the thrill and intensity of the octagon.

Chapter 104: Generational Clashes in the UFC

The UFC, throughout its storied history, has witnessed fighters from different generations stepping into the octagon to test their skills against each other. These battles of the ages often provide fans with captivating storylines and a unique glimpse into the evolution of mixed martial arts. In this chapter, we'll explore some of these memorable generational clashes.

Royce Gracie vs. Matt Hughes - UFC 60: Two Legends, Two Eras

One of the most iconic generational clashes in UFC history occurred at UFC 60 when the legendary Royce Gracie, one of the sport's early pioneers, faced off against Matt Hughes, a dominant champion of the modern era. This fight symbolized the changing face of MMA, with Gracie representing the sport's roots in Brazilian Jiu-Jitsu and Hughes showcasing the new breed of well-rounded fighters.

Randy Couture vs. Brock Lesnar - UFC 91: The Natural vs. The Beast

UFC 91 witnessed a showdown between Randy "The Natural" Couture, a veteran with extensive experience, and the imposing Brock Lesnar, a former WWE superstar transitioning into MMA. Couture's technical prowess clashed with Lesnar's raw athleticism, highlighting the sport's evolving skill sets and the importance of adaptability.

Anderson Silva vs. Israel Adesanya - UFC 234: The Spider vs. The Last Stylebender

In a battle that transcended eras, Anderson "The Spider" Silva, considered one of the greatest middleweights of all time, faced Israel "The Last Stylebender" Adesanya, an emerging talent with a unique fighting style. This fight showcased the passing of the torch from an MMA legend to a rising star and demonstrated the sport's continuous evolution.

Rich Franklin vs. Cung Le - UFC on Fuel TV 6: Old School vs. New School

Rich "Ace" Franklin, a former middleweight champion, clashed with Cung Le, known for his striking skills and cinematic martial arts background. This fight represented the meeting of traditional martial arts with modern MMA, emphasizing the diversity of techniques in the sport.

Glover Teixeira vs. Thiago Santos - UFC Fight Night 182: Veterans in the Spotlight

Glover Teixeira and Thiago Santos, both seasoned fighters, squared off in a matchup that showcased the enduring competitive spirit of veterans. Their battle was a testament to the physical and mental resilience required to excel in the UFC, regardless of age.

The Changing of the Guard

These generational clashes underscore the ever-changing landscape of the UFC. They provide fans with memorable moments that highlight the sport's evolution, from its early days characterized by specialization to the modern era where well-roundedness is paramount. As MMA continues to grow, so too will the narratives of fighters from different generations, creating a rich tapestry of stories within the octagon.

Legacy and Inspiration

The UFC's history is filled with generational clashes that define the sport's evolution. These fights not only entertain but also inspire future fighters to learn from the past while pushing the boundaries of what is possible in the cage. As long as the UFC continues to evolve, so too will the narratives of fighters from different generations, ensuring that the octagon remains a stage where legacies are forged and rewritten.

Chapter 105: Joe Son - From Hollywood Villain to Real-Life Antagonist

In the realm of Hollywood villains, there have been few as memorable as Joe Son. He made his debut as "Random Task" in the comedy film "Austin Powers: International Man of Mystery" in 1997. Portraying a parody of the James Bond character Oddjob, Son's role left a mark on popular culture, but not all that glitters is gold.

Evil Beyond the Screen

While Joe Son played the part of a villain on screen, his real-life actions were far more sinister. In 2008, he found himself in legal trouble that went beyond the world of cinema.

Criminal Convictions

Joe Son's descent into criminality began with an incident in 2008 when he was convicted of felony vandalism for an act of graffiti. However, this was only the tip of the iceberg.

The Disturbing Crime

What escalated matters from vandalism to a disturbing crime was a subsequent conviction. Joe Son was found guilty of participating in a gang rape in 1990. This heinous act came to light years later, and he was subsequently charged, tried, and sentenced to prison.

Imprisonment and Further Charges

While serving time for his involvement in the gang rape case, Joe Son faced additional charges. These charges stemmed from the murder of his cellmate in 2011. Son was accused of killing his cellmate in a gruesome manner. These shocking events showcased a far darker side of the man who had once portrayed a comedic henchman on the big screen.

The Legal Fallout

Joe Son's actions led to multiple convictions, ensuring that he would spend a considerable portion of his life behind bars. His criminal record and the notoriety surrounding his case would forever overshadow his brief stint in Hollywood.

A Dark Legacy

In the annals of Hollywood and real-life crime, Joe Son's story is a sobering reminder that appearances can be deceiving. While he left an indelible mark as Random Task in "Austin Powers," his subsequent actions and convictions paint a much darker picture. The world of entertainment may have been his first stage, but it was far from the last.

The Complex Legacy of Joe Son

In recounting the tale of Joe Son, it becomes evident that his life took a dark and tragic turn. From the bright lights of Hollywood to the confines of prison, his legacy serves as a stark reminder that real-life villains can be far more chilling than anything portrayed on the silver screen. While his role as Random Task may have made audiences laugh, the crimes he committed and the consequences he faced are no laughing matter.

Legacy and Reflection

The story of Joe Son is a cautionary tale that bridges the gap between Hollywood fantasy and the harsh realities of life. It reminds us that individuals are complex, capable of both good and evil, and that the line between fiction and reality can sometimes blur in the most unsettling ways. Joe Son's legacy serves as a reminder of the importance of distinguishing between the roles actors play and the choices they make in their own lives.

Chapter 106: Deciphering GSP's Chest Tattoo

Georges St-Pierre, widely known as GSP, is not only one of the greatest fighters in the history of the UFC but also an enigmatic figure with a distinctive chest tattoo that has piqued the curiosity of fans and analysts alike. In a 2007 interview, the welterweight champ shed some light on the ink that adorns his chest.

The Cryptic Tattoo

GSP's tattoo is a prominent feature that sits right in the center of his chest. For years, fans speculated about its meaning, prompting GSP to finally reveal its significance in the aforementioned interview.

Dual Nature

In his own words, GSP explained, "The tattoo on my chest means that there are two sides to me. I can be very rude, and I can be very nice. I like to be rude when I fight." This statement gives us a glimpse into the mindset of this exceptional fighter.

The Fighter's Dichotomy

GSP's characterization of his tattoo as representing a duality in his personality is intriguing. It suggests that inside the Octagon, he transforms into a fierce and relentless warrior, while outside of it, he returns to being a courteous and amicable individual.

The Rude Warrior

GSP's willingness to embrace a "rude" persona during his fights might be seen as a testament to his competitive spirit and the intensity he brings to his craft. It's a quality that has endeared him to fans who appreciate his dedication to the sport.

The Nice Guy Outside the Cage

Conversely, outside the cage, GSP is often described as a respectful and humble person. This stark contrast between his in-cage and out-of-cage personas is part of what makes him such a compelling figure in the world of mixed martial arts.

The Tattoo's Legacy

GSP's chest tattoo has become an iconic symbol of his career. It serves as a visual representation of the duality he embraces, reminding us that athletes like him can be multifaceted individuals with layers beyond what we see in the Octagon.

The Enigma of GSP

In deciphering GSP's chest tattoo, we are given a rare glimpse into the mindset of a fighter who has left an indelible mark on the UFC and the sport of mixed martial arts. His ability to channel his "rude" side when necessary, while remaining a "nice" guy outside of competition, showcases the complexity of his character.

A Living Legend

Georges St-Pierre's chest tattoo represents more than just ink on skin; it symbolizes the duality of his character as a fighter. His ability to seamlessly transition between being "rude" in the Octagon and "nice" in everyday life is a testament to his versatility and the enduring legacy he has crafted in the world of mixed martial arts.

Chapter 107: Fighters Under Scrutiny - Post-Fight Conduct

Mixed martial arts has grown immensely in popularity, thanks in part to the colorful personalities and intense rivalries that characterize the sport. However, with this fame and notoriety come expectations of professionalism and sportsmanship. Over the years, several fighters have faced criticism for their post-fight conduct, often overshadowing their in-cage achievements.

The High Stakes of Victory and Defeat

In the world of professional fighting, every bout carries significant stakes. Fighters invest countless hours in training, and their careers can be defined by their performance inside the cage. These high stakes, coupled with the adrenaline rush of competition, can sometimes lead to post-fight conduct that raises eyebrows.

Excessive Celebrations

One aspect of post-fight conduct that has drawn criticism is excessive celebrations. While it's natural for fighters to express their emotions after a hard-fought victory, some have taken it to extremes. Celebrations that involve taunting or disrespecting a fallen opponent have been met with backlash from fans, fellow fighters, and even regulatory bodies.

Confrontations and Brawls

Another post-fight issue that has garnered attention is physical confrontations outside of the cage. MMA is a sport where emotions run high, and rivalries can be intensely personal. In some cases, fighters have engaged in brawls with their opponents or their opponents' cornermen after the fight has officially ended. These incidents not only tarnish the sport's image but can also result in fines, suspensions, or legal consequences.

Trash Talk and Verbal Altercations

Verbal warfare has become an integral part of promoting MMA bouts. Fighters often engage in pre-fight trash talk to hype up their contests and generate interest among fans. However, when this trash talk continues after the fight, it can cross a line. Verbal altercations at post-fight interviews or press conferences have led to uncomfortable moments and negative publicity.

Regulatory Responses

MMA organizations and regulatory bodies have responded to instances of controversial post-fight conduct. Many have implemented codes of conduct and sportsmanship guidelines for fighters, emphasizing the importance of respecting opponents and maintaining professionalism. Fines, suspensions, or the withholding of bonuses are potential consequences for fighters who violate these guidelines.

Redemption and Lessons Learned

While some fighters continue to face criticism for their post-fight conduct, others have used these experiences as opportunities for growth and redemption. They have publicly acknowledged their mistakes, expressed remorse, and taken steps to improve their behavior. This willingness to learn from past actions is a testament to the maturation and personal development of many MMA athletes.

The Ongoing Challenge

The issue of post-fight conduct remains an ongoing challenge in the MMA world. The sport's organizers, fighters, and fans must strike a delicate balance between the intense emotions that drive the sport and the expectations of professionalism and sportsmanship. As MMA continues to evolve and gain mainstream acceptance, it is likely that the scrutiny of fighters' conduct, both inside and outside the cage, will only intensify.

In the Spotlight

The spotlight on fighters' post-fight conduct serves as a reminder that athletes in combat sports are not only judged by their physical abilities but also by their actions and behavior as representatives of the sport. Balancing the demands of competition with the expectations of sportsmanship remains a central theme in the ever-evolving world of MMA.

Chapter 108: Zuffa - More Than Just a Name

In the world of mixed martial arts, Zuffa is a name that holds significant meaning. It's not just a random combination of letters; rather, it has a cultural and linguistic connection. Zuffa, which translates to "scuffle" in Italian, is more than just the name of an MMA promotion company; it represents the essence of the sport.

The Birth of Zuffa

Zuffa was founded by casino executives Frank Fertitta III and Lorenzo Fertitta in 2001. The brothers had a vision of reviving and rebranding the struggling Ultimate Fighting Championship (UFC), which they purchased for $2 million. They recognized the potential of MMA as a sport that could captivate audiences worldwide.

Zuffa's Mission

From the beginning, Zuffa's mission was clear: to transform the UFC into a legitimate and respected sport. They aimed to take MMA out of the shadows and into the mainstream. The choice of the name "Zuffa" was not arbitrary but rather a reflection of their determination to elevate the sport.

Zuffa's Cultural Connection

The Italian word "Zuffa" means "scuffle" or "brawl," and it carries a sense of physicality and raw competition. By adopting this name, Zuffa embraced the essence of MMA itself. The sport is about two athletes engaging in a physical battle, a scuffle, inside the Octagon. It's about the struggle for dominance, the clash of wills, and the pursuit of victory.

Changing Perceptions

In the early days of the UFC, the sport faced significant challenges. It was often perceived as a spectacle, more akin to a no-holds-barred fight than a legitimate athletic competition. Zuffa's commitment to rebranding and promoting the sport as a disciplined, regulated, and professional endeavor was evident.

Elevating the UFC

Under Zuffa's leadership, the UFC implemented a series of changes. They introduced weight classes and unified rules, making the sport safer and more structured. They worked diligently to secure regulatory approval in various states, lifting the stigma associated with MMA.

The Ultimate Scuffle

The Octagon, where UFC fights take place, embodies the concept of a "scuffle." Inside that cage, fighters engage in the ultimate scuffle, testing their skills, courage, and determination. Zuffa's choice of name encapsulated the essence of the sport's appeal—a raw, unscripted battle.

The Legacy of Zuffa

In 2016, Zuffa sold the UFC for a staggering $4 billion to talent agency WME-IMG. While the Fertitta brothers' era as owners came to an end, their legacy lives on. Zuffa's contribution to MMA's transformation from a fringe spectacle to a global phenomenon is undeniable.

Zuffa, the Italian word for "scuffle," is a name deeply intertwined with the history and evolution of the UFC and MMA. It symbolizes the sport's essence—a raw, unbridled battle between two competitors striving for victory. The choice of this name by the Fertitta brothers and their dedication to transforming the sport have left an indelible mark on the world of mixed martial arts.

Chapter 109: Tito Ortiz - Unveiling the Real Name

In the world of mixed martial arts, fighters often adopt stage names or nicknames that resonate with their persona inside the cage. One such fighter is the legendary Tito Ortiz. While he's widely known by this name, his real identity is Jacob Christopher Ortiz. This chapter delves into the intriguing story behind Tito Ortiz's real name.

The Transformation to Tito Ortiz

Born on January 23, 1975, in Huntington Beach, California, Jacob Christopher Ortiz grew up in a challenging environment. As a young man, he discovered wrestling, which ultimately paved the way for his entry into the world of MMA. Early in his career, he adopted the moniker "Tito," a Spanish nickname meaning "uncle" or "buddy," which was given to him by his father.

The Rise of Tito Ortiz

Under the name Tito Ortiz, Jacob Christopher found tremendous success in the MMA world. He became one of the most recognizable and dominant fighters in the UFC's light heavyweight division during the late '90s and early 2000s. Known for his aggressive wrestling style and ground-and-pound tactics, Tito Ortiz defended his title multiple times and became a household name in the sport.

Behind the Scenes

While Tito Ortiz was a fierce and imposing figure inside the cage, Jacob Christopher Ortiz was a man with a multifaceted life outside of it. He was not just a fighter; he was also a loving father, a businessman, and a community leader.

The Ortiz Legacy

Tito Ortiz's real name, Jacob Christopher Ortiz, represents the duality of a fighter's life. It highlights the distinction between the persona in the cage and the individual outside of it. Throughout his career, Tito Ortiz made significant contributions to the sport, and his legacy continues to inspire aspiring fighters.

A New Beginning

In recent years, Tito Ortiz has embarked on a new journey, transitioning into a post-fighting career. He's ventured into politics, becoming the Mayor Pro Tem of Huntington Beach, California. This transition showcases the versatility and resilience of Jacob Christopher Ortiz beyond the realm of MMA.

While the world knows him as Tito Ortiz, the fighter, it's essential to remember that every fighter has a real identity beyond their stage name. Jacob Christopher Ortiz's transformation from a troubled youth to a legendary MMA champion and community leader is a testament to the power of dedication and perseverance.

Chapter 110: A Toothsome Proposition

In the annals of mixed martial arts history, certain moments become iconic, forever etched in the minds of fans and fighters alike. One such moment occurred at UFC 1 when Gerard Gordeau faced Telia Tuli, and in a mere 30 seconds, the sport was changed forever. This chapter uncovers the remarkable story behind that fight, where not only teeth flew but also embedded themselves in an unexpected place.

The Historic Showdown

UFC 1, held on November 12, 1993, marked the birth of the Ultimate Fighting Championship. Eight fighters from various disciplines gathered to test their skills in a tournament that had no rules, no weight classes, and no-holds-barred combat.

Gordeau, a Dutch karate and kickboxing specialist, faced off against Telia Tuli, a Hawaiian sumo wrestler, in one of the inaugural bouts. The match is most remembered for its brevity, as Gordeau knocked out Tuli in a blistering 30 seconds.

The Flying Tooth

While the swift knockout itself was extraordinary, it was a seemingly mundane result of the kick that added to the fight's legend. One of Tuli's teeth was dislodged from his mouth by the force of Gordeau's strike, launching it into the audience. It became an instant talking point among spectators and commentators.

The Hidden Challenge

What most fans may not know is that the story didn't end there. According to Erich Krauss's book "Brawl," two more of Tuli's teeth didn't just fall out but became lodged in Gordeau's foot. This bizarre turn of events was a testament to the raw and unpredictable nature of early MMA.

The Consequences

Rather than extracting the embedded teeth from Gordeau's foot in the cage, doctors decided against it to avoid the risk of an open wound. This decision led to an unexpected series of events. Gordeau, undeterred by the discomfort, went on to fight twice more that night, including a memorable encounter with Royce Gracie in the final.

The Infection

Unfortunately for Gordeau, the aftermath of this historic night was far from glamorous. The wounds caused by the embedded teeth became severely infected. When he returned home, he had to undergo weeks of medical treatment to address the consequences of those surreal moments inside the Octagon.

The tale of Gerard Gordeau's toothsome encounter with Telia Tuli at UFC 1 is a vivid reminder of the sport's wild and unpredictable early days. It showcases the extraordinary circumstances that fighters faced and their unwavering determination to compete, even when faced with unexpected challenges like embedded teeth in the foot. This strange but compelling chapter in UFC history is one that fans and fighters alike will never forget.

Chapter 111: Dana White Never Had a Pro Boxing Fight

Dana White is a name synonymous with mixed martial arts (MMA). As the President of the Ultimate Fighting Championship (UFC), he's one of the most influential figures in combat sports. However, despite his deep involvement in the fight game, there's an interesting fact about him – he's never had a professional boxing match. This chapter delves into Dana White's background and why he chose not to step into the boxing ring professionally.

Dana White: The MMA Mogul

Before he became the face of the UFC, Dana White had a diverse career that included managing fighters and boxers. He grew up in a rough neighborhood in Boston, where he learned to be street-smart and resilient. These qualities would serve him well in the world of combat sports.

From Boxing to UFC

In the early 2000s, White was instrumental in transitioning the UFC from a niche spectacle to a mainstream sport. His vision and leadership helped elevate the organization, turning it into a global powerhouse. While he promoted countless MMA fights, his experience with boxing was limited to managing a few fighters.

Why Dana White Never Stepped In

White's decision not to have a professional boxing match may seem curious, considering his deep involvement in combat sports. Several factors likely influenced this choice:

Business Focus: Dana White recognized that his real talent lay in promotion and business. He understood the fight game, but he wasn't a fighter himself. Instead, he focused on building the UFC brand into what it is today.

Risk and Injury: Professional boxing is a demanding and grueling sport. Stepping into the ring as a fighter carries the risk of serious injury. White may have chosen not to take this risk, considering his role as the face of the UFC.

Promoter's Role: White's passion lay in promoting fights and building stars. He found fulfillment in managing fighters and putting together matchups that excited fans. This role allowed him to shape the sport without having to be an active competitor.

Dana White's Influence on Boxing

While Dana White never had a professional boxing match, his impact on the sport extends beyond MMA. In recent years, he's ventured into boxing promotion, including the highly publicized crossover bout between Floyd Mayweather Jr. and Conor McGregor. White's involvement in the boxing world showcases his adaptability and ambition.

Dana White's decision not to step into the professional boxing ring may have surprised some, but it aligns with his strengths and passions. His journey from a Boston neighborhood to the pinnacle of MMA and his forays into boxing promotion illustrate that there's more than one way to leave an indelible mark on the combat sports world. White's legacy is firmly established as a promoter and businessman, rather than as a fighter, and that's a role he's excelled in for decades.

Closing Thoughts

Our exploration of the UFC's vibrant history and fascinating intricacies has been nothing short of thrilling. We embarked on this journey to uncover the weird, fun, and random facts that have woven themselves into the fabric of this extraordinary sport. As we wrap up this literary octagon odyssey, let's take a moment to dive deeper into some of the key themes that emerged throughout our exploration.

A Glimpse into the UFC's Past and Present

We began our journey by delving into the annals of UFC history. From the inaugural event in Denver, Colorado, to the meteoric rise of stars like Royce Gracie and Ken Shamrock, we witnessed the sport's transformation from a niche spectacle to a global phenomenon.

The UFC's commitment to innovation and adaptation has been a constant theme. We witnessed the evolution of the sport from the early days of no-holds-barred contests to the highly regulated and safety-focused competitions of today. Through controversies, rule changes, and strategic acquisitions, the UFC has consistently demonstrated its ability to adapt and thrive.

The Legends of the Octagon: Athletic Prowess and Sportsmanship

Our journey through the UFC's rich tapestry introduced us to legendary fighters like Anderson Silva and Georges St-Pierre. These athletes showcased not only exceptional skills within the cage but also a level of sportsmanship and dignity that resonated with fans worldwide.

The emergence of modern-day icons such as Conor McGregor and Ronda Rousey served as a testament to the UFC's ability to reinvent itself through charismatic and dynamic athletes. Their stories, filled with triumphs and setbacks, offered a glimpse into the incredible dedication and sacrifices required to succeed in the world's toughest sport.

The UFC Beyond the Octagon: Global Reach and Fighter Safety

The UFC's expansion beyond the confines of the octagon was another captivating facet of our exploration. We traveled the globe with the UFC, discovering events held in iconic venues like Madison Square Garden and exploring the unique challenges posed by outdoor arenas. The partnership with the United States Anti-Doping Agency (USADA) underscored the organization's unwavering commitment to fighter safety and fair competition.

We also uncovered the lesser-known elements of the UFC, from its presence on social media platforms to its dedication to fighter safety through a specialized medical staff. The UFC's own merchandise line and the glitzy Hall of Fame induction ceremonies added layers to our understanding of the sport's cultural impact.

Behind the Scenes and Beyond the Cage: The UFC's Multifaceted World

Our journey took us behind the scenes of UFC media coverage, revealing the drama and theatrics of pre-fight trash talk that often precedes epic bouts. We explored the transition of fighters into the realms of acting and entertainment, showcasing their versatility and ambition beyond the octagon.

Unusual, Quirky, and Surprising: Traversing the Unexpected

Among the wealth of information, we stumbled upon some truly unusual, quirky, and surprising facts. From deciphering the meaning behind Georges St-Pierre's tattoo to the toothy aftermath of a historic UFC 1 fight, these tidbits added an element of whimsy to our exploration.

Conclusion: Celebrating the UFC's Endless Stories

As we bring this journey to a close, it's essential to acknowledge that the UFC is not just about fights in the octagon; it's a tapestry of stories, characters, and moments. It's the underdog triumphing against the odds; it's the relentless pursuit of excellence, the dedication, and the sacrifices made to reach the pinnacle of the sport.

The UFC's allure lies not only in the fierce battles within the cage but in the extraordinary individuals who step into it. It's the camaraderie of fans, the anticipation of each fight night, and the shared moments that create lasting memories.

This book, "111 Weird, Fun, and Random Facts about the UFC," has been a celebration of those moments, a testament to the rich history and boundless potential of mixed martial arts. As we conclude this exploration, we look forward to the continued evolution of the UFC and the countless stories that are yet to be written in the annals of this remarkable sport.

In the spirit of sportsmanship and camaraderie,

James Bren

Other Books by James Bren

The History of MMA

The History of the NFL

The History of the NHL and the Stanley Cup

The History of the UFC – Book 1

The History of the UFC – Book 2. *Coming soon!*

Made in United States
Troutdale, OR
12/19/2023